BLUEPRINTS

Geography
Key Stage 1
Teacher's Resource
Book

Stephen Scoffham

176

Colin Bridge

Terry Jewson

Stanley Thornes (Publishers) Ltd

BLUEPRINTS – HOW TO GET MORE INFORMATION

Blueprints is an expanding series of practical teacher's ideas books and photocopiable resources for use in primary schools. Books are available for every Key Stage of every core and foundation subject, as well as for an ever widening range of other primary needs. **Blueprints** are carefully structured around the demands of National Curriculum but may be used successfully by schools and teachers not following the National Curriculum in England and Wales.

Blueprints provide:

- Total National Curriculum coverage
- Hundreds of practical ideas
- Books specifically for the Key Stage you teach
- Flexible resources for the whole school or for individual teachers
- Excellent photocopiable sheets – ideal for assessment, SATs and children's work profiles
- Supreme value.

Books may be bought by credit card over the telephone and information obtained on (0242) 228888. Alternatively, photocopy and return this FREEPOST form to join our mailing list. We will mail you regularly with information on new and existing titles.

Please add my name to the BLUEPRINTS mailing list.   *Photocopiable*

Name _____

Address_____

_____

_____

Postcode_____

To: Marketing Services Dept., Stanley Thornes Publishers, FREEPOST (GR 782), Cheltenham, Glos. GL53 1BR

Text © Stephen Scoffham, Colin Bridge, Terry Jewson 1992
Illustrations by Linda Herd © ST(P) Ltd 1992

Statements of Attainment and Programmes of Study for Key Stage 1 are reproduced with the permission of the Controller of Her Majesty's Stationery Office.

First published in 1992 by:
Stanley Thornes (Publishers) Ltd
Ellenborough House
Wellington Street
CHELTENHAM GL50 1YD

Reprinted 1993 (twice)

A catalogue record for this book is available from the British Library.

ISBN 0–7487–1349–2

Typeset by Tech-Set, Gateshead, Tyne & Wear.
Printed and bound in Great Britain at The Bath Press, Avon.

CONTENTS

INTRODUCTION

The geography curriculum

Since September 1991 teachers in England and Wales have been required by law to teach geography to children in state-maintained schools. The geography National Curriculum specifies Statements of Attainment against which children will be assessed. It also prescribes Programmes of Study for children at each Key Stage. Teachers are expected to use their professional judgement in determining how best to deliver these requirements. However, the National Curriculum Council has published Non-Statutory Guidance which gives advice on a number of important topics.

The geography curriculum is divided into five Attainment Targets:

Attainment Target 1 Geographical skills
Attainment Target 2 Knowledge and understanding of places
Attainment Target 3 Physical geography
Attainment Target 4 Human geography
Attainment Target 5 Environmental geography.

These Attainment Targets can be combined in a variety of different ways. There are also good opportunities for linking geographical studies with other curriculum areas.

Key Stage 1

The Programme of Study for Key Stage 1 specifies the work that children should undertake in the infant school. It emphasises the enquiry method in which children conduct their own investigations, based on both fieldwork and classroom activities. It also lists the different places which children have to study. These are:

- the local area
- a contrasting locality in the United Kingdom
- a locality beyond the United Kingdom.

A locality is defined as 'a small area with distinctive features', and the local area as either 'the immediate vicinity of the school' or the vicinity 'where the pupil lives'.

This is the first time that infants have been required to undertake geographical studies. The National Curriculum should help to ensure that by the time they reach the junior school, children will have a basis of geographical knowledge and understanding. It is an exciting challenge. This book outlines some of the ways in which it can be met.

HOW TO USE THIS BOOK

What is *Blueprints Geography?*

Blueprints Geography Key Stage 1 has been devised to cover all the requirements of the geography National Curriculum at Key Stage 1. It consists of this *Teacher's Resource Book*, which may be used independently, and an accompanying book of *Pupils' Copymasters*. It is intended for practising teachers, particularly non-specialists who may find themselves teaching geography for the first time in their career. Students and others who are involved with education will also find it invaluable.

The *Teacher's Resource Book* contains over 300 ideas and practical suggestions. There is a particularly strong emphasis on mapwork, fieldwork and locality studies. These are developed and extended in the supporting book of *Pupils' Copymasters*.

How is the *Teacher's Resource Book* organised?

The *Teacher's Resource Book* is divided into five sections, one for each Attainment Target. There is a general introduction and background notes at the beginning of each section. This is followed by a resource bank of activities for Levels 1 and 2, and a chart which suggests work for Level 3. The Level 3 activities have not been developed in detail, partly because only a minority of children will require them, and partly because there is a wealth of ideas for Level 3 in *Blueprints Geography Key Stage 2*.

The *Teacher's Resource Book* also follows the structure of the National Curriculum. Each section covers an Attainment Target, and is divided into areas of study based on a particular Statement of Attainment. This approach means that the activities are easy to locate and are graded into National Curriculum levels.

How can I select activities for my class?

You can use *Blueprints Geography* as a flexible resource which you can consult in a number of different ways:

1 You can work from the topic planner and web diagrams on pages 7–27. These have been selected to give full coverage of the geography curriculum, and group together activities from different parts of the book. There are also suggestions for cross-curricular links.

2 You can identify areas of the geography curriculum which you wish to teach, and turn directly to the appropriate area of study. There are at least half a dozen activities for each Statement of Attainment, plus supporting copymasters.

3 You can select activities of your choice to support an individual programme of work. The topic planner and area of study headings will help you to locate them easily.

How do I use the copymasters?

In the accompanying book of copymasters, there are generally three or four copymasters for each Statement of Attainment. You will find the relevant copymasters referred to with this symbol: and they are listed at the end of each area of study, with instructions on how to use them. You can complete most of the activities without using the copymasters, but they will allow you to develop the activities to their full potential. They are particularly important in developing the enquiry and fieldwork skills required by the National Curriculum.

What records should I keep?

It is important that you keep a record of the children's work so that you can monitor their progress. One way of doing this is to keep a folder for each child. The copymasters provide an ideal and easy way of building up a record of experiences in National Curriculum geography. Another way of monitoring progress is to record the different activities that the children have completed on a class master list. More detailed advice on assessment and record keeping is given below. There is also a photocopiable record sheet based on the requirements of the National Curriculum overleaf.

What resources will I need?

You will need to build up a bank of resources in order to teach National Curriculum geography. Large-scale Ordnance Survey maps of the local area are invaluable. Globes, atlases, photographs, fieldwork equipment and computer programs will also be required. There is a list of addresses of appropriate agencies and commercial suppliers on page 132. The resources required for each activity are listed at the beginning of the activity.

ASSESSMENT ▶

Assessment in geography at Key Stage 1 will be based entirely on tasks set by the teacher. These could take a variety of forms, from simple written tests and mapwork exercises to fieldwork investigations.

Whatever the format, you will need to check that the children can understand instructions, use geographical vocabulary and talk with confidence about what they are doing. It is crucial that children are given the opportunity to conduct their own enquiries and arrive at independent conclusions. In due course a number of Standard Assessment Tasks (SATs) will be drawn up to provide examples. When these appear they should help you to devise tasks of your own.

Records of achievement

If you have used the copymasters that accompany this book, you may decide to use them in assessment. Many of the sheets require children to collect information, make choices and analyse the results in a simple way. Completed sheets can be stored and used as a record of achievement.

You may also want to use the record sheet overleaf. This lists the Statements of Attainment at Levels 1 and 2. By putting a mark against each Statement it will be possible to see what each child has accomplished. If the sheet is completed at regular intervals it will trace the child's progress from year to year.

By keeping proper records you will be able to identify achievements and learning difficulties. Nowadays teachers are obliged to show what children have accomplished. If you have a well-organised system this does not have to be a daunting task.

GEOGRAPHY RECORD SHEET		Name	Year		
			R	1	2
AT1		1a) Follow directions			
		1b) Talk about a familiar place			
		2a) Use geographical vocabulary			
		2b) Represent places on a map			
		2c) Follow a route			
		2d) Record the weather			
		2e) Interpret photographs			
AT2		1a) Name local features			
		1b) Activities in the local area			
		1c) State where they live			
		1d) The wider world			
		1e) Name their own country			
		2a) Name countries of the United Kingdom			
		2b) Describe local land use			
		2c) A contrasting locality			
		2d) Compare localities			
AT3		1a) Rock, soil and water			
		2a) Weather and seasons			
		2b) Water in the environment			
AT4		1a) Uses of different buildings			
		1b) Ways people travel			
		1c) Different kinds of work			
		2a) Homes and settlements			
		2b) Reasons for journeys			
		2c) Provision of goods and services			
AT5		1a) Name materials			
		1b) Personal likes and dislikes			
		2a) Obtaining natural materials			
		2b) Changing the environment			
		2c) Improve the environment			

You may wish to teach geography through topics, and to integrate it with other subject areas. If you decide to do this, it will be important to ensure that you obtain a full and balanced coverage of the curriculum.

The matrix below shows how selected topics relate to the geography Attainment Targets. The topics have been chosen because they deliver all the requirements of the curriculum at Key Stage 1. Most of the topics combine a number of different Attainment Targets. There is a brief description of each topic, together with web diagrams and references to supporting activities, in the planners on pages 8–27.

Topic	Level	Attainment Targets 1	2	3	4	5
Ourselves and school	1	•	•			
	2	•				
	3	•				
Homes and families	1	•	•		•	
	2					
	3					
Moving around	1	•			•	
	2	•			•	
	3	•			•	
Where we live	1		•		•	•
	2		•			
	3		•			
Water	1			•		
	2			•		
	3			•		

Topic	Level	Attainment Targets 1	2	3	4	5
Weather	1					
	2	•		•		
	3			•		
People at work	1				•	
	2				•	
	3		•			
Villages and towns	1					
	2		•		•	
	3				•	
Other lands	1		•			
	2	•	•			
	3		•			
The countryside	1					•
	2					•
	3					•

Schemes of work

In selecting your topics you will need to construct a scheme which:

- allows children to progress from level to level
- relates to the curriculum plan for your school
- provides opportunities for enquiries and fieldwork
- makes the best use of available teaching resources.

The chart below shows one possible structure. It allows children in the reception class to draw extensively on their own experience and interests. At the same time it gives children in year 2 access to higher levels of enquiry.

Year	Topic		
R	Ourselves and school	Homes and families	Moving around
1	Where we live	Water	Weather
2	People at work	Other lands	The countryside

OURSELVES AND SCHOOL

'Ourselves' is a popular primary school topic. Young children feel comfortable and secure when thinking about themselves and their possessions. They are usually keen to talk about what they can do and are interested in comparing their belongings and personal accomplishments with other children of a similar age.

As they think about their bodies, children will naturally be led to consider their basic needs, such as food, clothing and the provision of goods and services. The study of the school building will raise questions about materials and protection from the weather. Not only does this link geography and science, it also provides natural opportunities for reading and artwork.

'Places to play' introduces the idea of leisure and recreation, while 'journey to school' focuses on movement. Most children are also fascinated by school days of the past, which adds a historical dimension.

Geographical studies can make this topic much more rounded and balanced, and help children to understand their place in the world. There are also opportunities for simple fieldwork, and the beginnings of a local area study. You could walk the children around the school to look at materials, talk about the things they notice on their daily journeys and identify clues to the past. All these things add variety to the classroom experience and are an essential foundation for good geographical learning.

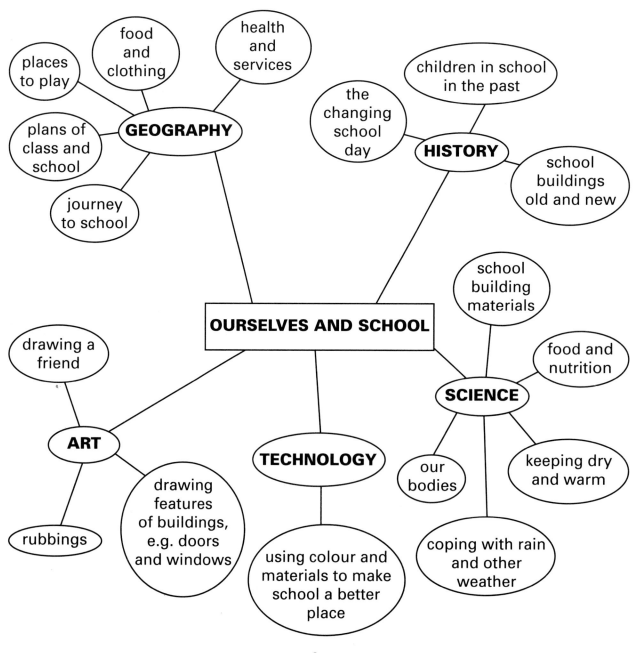

Ourselves and school – main Statements of Attainment

AT1 1b Pupils should be able to observe and talk about a familiar place.
AT1 2c Pupils should be able to follow a route using a plan.
AT2 1b Pupils should be able to identify activities carried out by people in the local area.

Related activities

Attainment Target 1
Activity 1.1   Direction words
Activity 1.7   Left and right survey
Activity 1.8   Direction finder
Activity 1.9   Mystery trail
Activity 1.11 Signs in school
Activity 1.13 Compass directions
Activity 1.16 Our school
Activity 1.17 School photo quiz
Activity 1.18 Teddy bear visit
Activity 1.19 Classroom windows
Activity 1.20 Different views
Activity 1.24 Personal feelings
Activity 1.34 Class plan
Activity 1.35 Signpost map
Activity 1.36 Journey plan
Activity 1.38 Adventure playground
Activity 1.41 Footprints
Activity 1.42 School journeys
Activity 1.43 Follow the route
Activity 1.44 Street trail

Attainment Target 2
Activity 2.9   School jobs
Activity 2.10 Job fact files
Activity 2.12 Running a school
Activity 2.16 Time to spare
Activity 2.58 Classroom areas
Activity 2.59 Areas in school
Activity 2.60 School walk
Activity 2.64 Games and pastimes

Attainment Target 3
Activity 3.7   Investigating the school grounds
Activity 3.20 Water walk
Activity 3.21 Playground quiz

Attainment Target 4
Activity 4.10 Getting to school survey
Activity 4.50 Emergency services
Activity 4.51 Services in schools

Attainment Target 5
Activity 5.3   Resources in the classroom
Activity 5.15 Things we like in school
Activity 5.16 Sensory walk
Activity 5.20 Different opinions
Activity 5.43 Classroom improvements
Activity 5.44 School improvements
Activity 5.49 Tree planting

HOMES AND FAMILIES

Young children quite naturally see the world in terms of the things which are familiar in their daily lives, and teaching strategies which are based on this interest tend to be particularly successful. 'Homes and Families' is an ideal topic for drawing on personal experiences. However, the work needs to be carefully planned if it is not simply to celebrate familiar events.

In geographical terms, this topic represents another stage in the child's early studies of the local area. It will involve recognising different types of homes, thinking about shopping patterns and comparing the needs of old and young people. The children will also need to look at the rhythm of family life and daily activities. The analysis of the immediate environment is a vital part of geography, and essential if children are to recognise as they grow older how their own area contrasts with distant places.

There are many opportunities for cross-curricular links. In history you could consider family life in the past. The changing nature of technology in the home introduces a scientific dimension. Models and collages can be created as part of a programme of work in art lessons.

Homes and families – main Statements of Attainment

AT1 1b Pupils should be able to observe and talk about a familiar place.
AT2 1b Pupils should be able to identify activities carried out by people in the local area.
AT2 1c Pupils should be able to state where they live.
AT4 1a Pupils should be able to recognise that buildings are used for different purposes.

Related activities

Attainment Target 1
Activity 1.18 Teddy bear visit
Activity 1.21 Streets and houses

Attainment Target 2
Activity 2.9   School jobs
Activity 2.10 Job fact files
Activity 2.11 Tools and equipment
Activity 2.12 Running a school
Activity 2.13 Advertisements
Activity 2.14 Street work
Activity 2.15 Mime a job
Activity 2.16 Time to spare
Activity 2.17 Envelopes
Activity 2.18 Your address
Activity 2.19 Animal addresses
Activity 2.20 House numbers
Activity 2.21 Front doors
Activity 2.22 Streets
Activity 2.23 Street names
Activity 2.24 Name rubbings
Activity 2.25 Post office
Activity 2.26 Letter post
Activity 2.27 Postcodes

Attainment Target 4
Activity 4.1   Different buildings
Activity 4.2   Name the parts
Activity 4.3   Rooms with a purpose
Activity 4.4   Building quiz
Activity 4.5   Comparing buildings
Activity 4.6   Places of work
Activity 4.7   Building survey
Activity 4.8   Buildings around the world
Activity 4.9   Fantasy houses
Activity 4.20 School jobs
Activity 4.21 People who help us
Activity 4.30 Where we live
Activity 4.31 Types of houses

Attainment Target 5
Activity 5.37 Obsolete objects

MOVING AROUND

Transport is a common infant school topic and there is little doubt that children enjoy finding out about different types of vehicles, such as steam engines, hot air balloons and sailing ships. However, it is important to ensure that geographical considerations are not obscured by an emphasis on history and vehicle technology. The topic web indicates how to plan for a more balanced approach.

There are many questions for children to investigate. Why do people travel? What routes do they take? How do drivers know where to go? How have vehicles changed? As well as using maps and reference material, there will be opportunities to use direct experience and to develop observations which the children have made for themselves while on journeys.

There is also considerable potential for work in science and technology. The children can design and test vehicles of their own. The problems of rough ground and uneven terrain present a special challenge. You might consider special vehicles such as Land-rovers and hovercraft. How do people move through air and water? What special machines have they devised to help them?

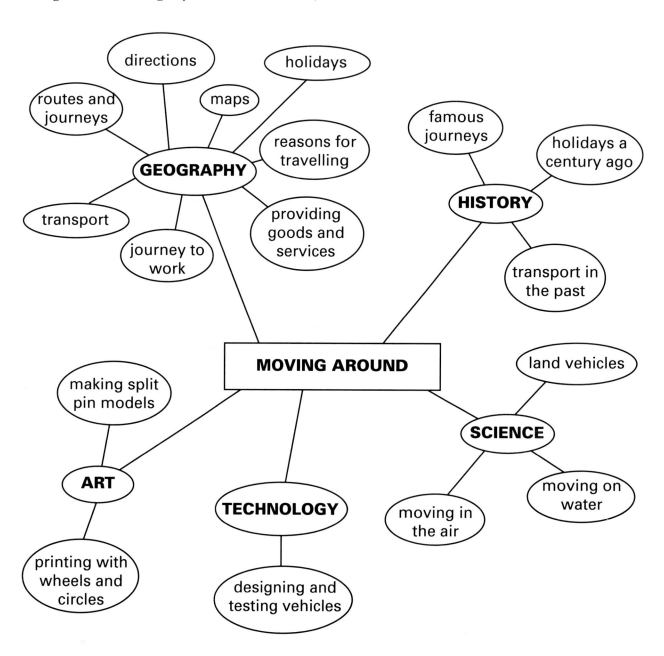

Moving around – main Statements of Attainment

AT1 1a Pupils should be able to follow directions.
AT1 2c Pupils should be able to follow a route using a plan.
AT4 1b Pupils should be able to describe ways in which people make journeys.
AT4 2b Pupils should be able to give reasons why people make journeys of different lengths.

Related activities

Attainment Target 1
Activity 1.1   Direction words
Activity 1.2   Blindfold donkey game
Activity 1.3   Model farm
Activity 1.4   Arrows
Activity 1.5   Left and right
Activity 1.6   Left and right stick
Activity 1.7   Left and right survey
Activity 1.8   Direction finder
Activity 1.9   Mystery trail
Activity 1.10 Programmable toy
Activity 1.11 Signs in school
Activity 1.12 Signs in the street
Activity 1.13 Compass directions
Activity 1.14 Make a compass
Activity 1.15 North and South Pole
Activity 1.31 Overhead projector
Activity 1.32 Plan views
Activity 1.33 Tray game
Activity 1.34 Class plan
Activity 1.35 Signpost map
Activity 1.36 Journey plan
Activity 1.41 Footprints
Activity 1.42 School journeys
Activity 1.43 Follow the route
Activity 1.44 Street trail
Activity 1.45 Direction signs
Activity 1.46 Journeys
Activity 1.47 On the road

Attainment Target 2
Activity 2.31 Holidays
Activity 2.32 Travellers
Activity 2.53 Connections
Activity 2.65 Roads

Attainment Target 3
Activity 3.6   Different surfaces

Attainment Target 4
Activity 4.10 Getting to school survey
Activity 4.11 Toy vehicles
Activity 4.12 Bus journeys
Activity 4.13 Transport survey
Activity 4.14 Vehicle collage
Activity 4.15 Holiday journeys
Activity 4.16 Obstacles
Activity 4.17 Famous journeys
Activity 4.18 Stories of journeys
Activity 4.39 Near or far?
Activity 4.40 Journey to school
Activity 4.41 Journeys around the school
Activity 4.42 Reasons for travel
Activity 4.43 Places to visit
Activity 4.44 Journeys for work
Activity 4.45 Journey survey
Activity 4.46 Holiday journeys
Activity 4.48 Adventure journeys

WHERE WE LIVE

One advantage of tackling a variety of topics with a geographical emphasis is that the topics reinforce each other and together give a balanced coverage of the curriculum. In addition, each topic provides different opportunities for fieldwork and investigations in the local area. When it comes to planning a local area study it is tempting to cover too much material. What is suggested here is a number of ideas restricted to the character and quality of the environment.

The children could begin by illustrating where they live in drawings, models and picture maps. Do they live in a village, town or city? What are the main buildings and places of interest? They might then go on to consider the underlying physical landforms and the way people have used the environment. At some point they should also discuss the things they like and dislike. Geography is about personal opinions as well as scientific facts.

Other areas of the curriculum are fairly easy to incorporate. A study of local history will help to reveal the special character of the area. It may be possible to bring this to life by asking elderly people to describe events, buildings and streets that they remember. Changes in vehicles and machinery will provide a link to science and technology. The natural habitat should also be considered, perhaps by visiting a park or nature reserve.

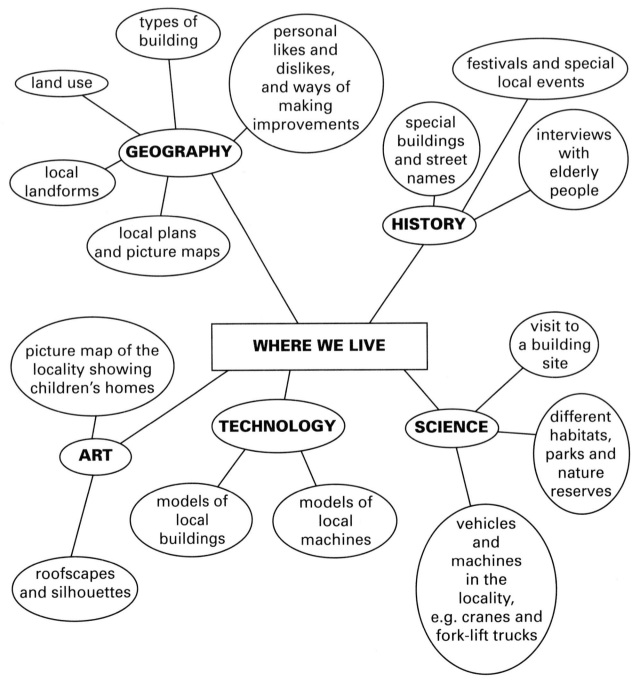

Where we live – main Statements of Attainment

AT2 1a Pupils should be able to name familiar features of the local area.
AT2 1e Pupils should be able to name the country in which they live.
AT2 2b Pupils should be able to describe uses of land and buildings in the local area.
AT4 1a Pupils should be able to recognise that buildings are used for different purposes.
AT5 1b Pupils should be able to express personal likes and dislikes about features of the local area.

Related activities

Attainment Target 1
Activity 1.22 Our locality
Activity 1.23 The neighbourhood
Activity 1.29 Picture maps
Activity 1.60 Familiar scenes
Activity 1.61 Fieldwork sketches

Attainment Target 2
Activity 2.1   Familiar features
Activity 2.2   Places snap
Activity 2.3   Picture map
Activity 2.4   Landmarks
Activity 2.5   Places alphabet
Activity 2.6   Guide book
Activity 2.7   Landmark models
Activity 2.8   Places quiz
Activity 2.38 Map exhibition
Activity 2.39 Name plates
Activity 2.40 Name display
Activity 2.41 Acrostic
Activity 2.42 Jigsaw puzzle
Activity 2.61 Different places
Activity 2.62 Selling things
Activity 2.63 Making things
Activity 2.64 Games and pastimes
Activity 2.65 Roads
Activity 2.66 Contrasts
Activity 2.76 Symbols

Attainment Target 3
Activity 3.8   At the park
Activity 3.9   Rocks in buildings

Attainment Target 4
Activity 4.1   Different buildings
Activity 4.5   Comparing buildings
Activity 4.7   Building survey
Activity 4.9   Fantasy houses
Activity 4.29 Street survey
Activity 4.31 Types of houses
Activity 4.33 Wall map
Activity 4.34 Photograph album

Attainment Target 5
Activity 5.15 Things we like in school
Activity 5.16 Sensory walk
Activity 5.17 Word game
Activity 5.18 The local environment
Activity 5.19 Different features
Activity 5.20 Different opinions
Activity 5.21 Likes and dislikes
Activity 5.22 Good for children
Activity 5.36 Change in your locality
Activity 5.39 Door walk
Activity 5.41 Favourite building
Activity 5.51 Improvements in the locality

WATER

Water is a popular topic throughout the primary school. One reason for this is that it covers a wide variety of different themes. Another reason is that it provides effective cross-curricular links. However, all-embracing topics of this kind run the risk of becoming too general. The web diagram adopts a much narrower focus by concentrating on the physical characteristics of water, to the exclusion of other considerations.

The project provides plenty of opportunities for simple fieldwork around the school. Where are the main pipes, taps and drains? Where does tap water come from and where does waste water go? This will lead naturally into an investigation of water in a variety of forms, such as rain, fog and frost.

Historical studies about clean water and the problems of disease represent another dimension. There is also the question of water supply in the modern world. This is something which affects people in many different countries, and so introduces a global dimension in a way that children can readily understand.

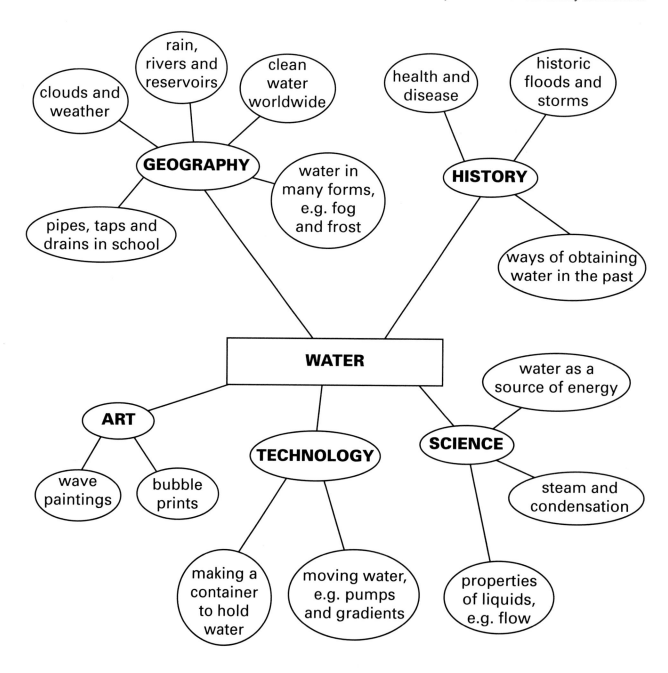

Water – main Statements of Attainment

AT3 1a Pupils should be able to recognise rocks, soil and water and understand that they are part of the environment.

AT3 2b Pupils should be able to identify the forms in which water occurs in the environment.

Related activities

Attainment Target 3
Activity 3.2   Feely box
Activity 3.3   Miniature garden
Activity 3.4   Looking at sand
Activity 3.5   Different soils
Activity 3.7   Investigating the school grounds
Activity 3.10 Seashore visit
Activity 3.17 Water experiments
Activity 3.18 Frozen water
Activity 3.19 Word mobile
Activity 3.20 Water walk
Activity 3.21 Playground quiz
Activity 3.22 Water and landscapes
Activity 3.23 Adventure story

WEATHER

The weather influences our daily lives and is of central importance to both geography and science. Many infant teachers will be familiar with this topic, which has been a favourite for many years. The web diagram illustrates the potential for integrated work across the curriculum.

In geography, children should record the weather over a short period of time. They should then consider the differences between the seasons and make comparisons with places around the world that show significant differences. Finally, they might discuss the way in which the weather affects plants, animals and people in their daily lives.

For a historical study of weather there are many pictures, stories and poems which describe how life followed the seasons in the past. There is a vivid and valuable link to geography in looking at historic natural disasters, such as floods or volcanic eruptions. Science can be pursued by finding out about the effects of light, heat and cold. There should be plenty of examples in the home and school of the way people have used these physical forces to their advantage, as well as the problems they can cause.

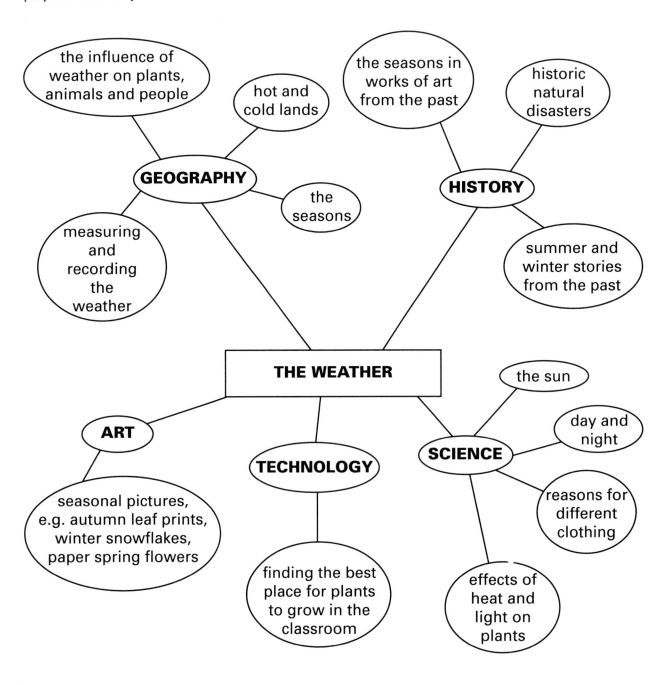

The weather – main Statements of Attainment

AT1 2d Pupils should be able to record weather observations made over a short period.
AT3 2a Pupils should be able to recognise seasonal weather patterns.

Related activities

Attainment Target 1
Activity 1.28 Word scales
Activity 1.48 Weather words
Activity 1.49 Weather symbols
Activity 1.50 Experiencing the weather
Activity 1.51 All in a day
Activity 1.52 Recording the weather
Activity 1.53 Weather dial
Activity 1.54 Weather forecast
Activity 1.55 The right weather
Activity 1.56 Wind testers
Activity 1.57 Weather picture
Activity 1.58 Weather music
Activity 1.59 World weather

Attainment Target 3
Activity 3.11 Dressed for the season
Activity 3.12 Musical moods
Activity 3.13 Season tree
Activity 3.14 Seasonal words
Activity 3.15 Poetry cube
Activity 3.16 Seasonal Cluedo

PEOPLE AT WORK

The notion that work is a distinct activity filters only slowly into a child's perception. For infants, life is a whole experience that is channelled by the occasional demands of adults. Play is a serious business, and events are not separated. A study of different jobs done in the community and the roles that adults fulfil can enlarge the children's understanding and capture their imagination.

There are many questions to consider. What jobs do adults do in your school? What things are made locally? What is the difference between goods and services? How do people get to work? Which jobs have to be done at night or at the weekend?

It is often rewarding to contrast current forms of employment with the work that people did in the past. You could highlight particular aspects by making a case study of a farm, shop or village community. Manufacturing processes provide an ideal way of introducing science and technology. One approach is to consider the stages involved in making an everyday object. Young children often find it hard to associate products with raw materials, and helping them to do so can prove to be a valuable piece of work in itself.

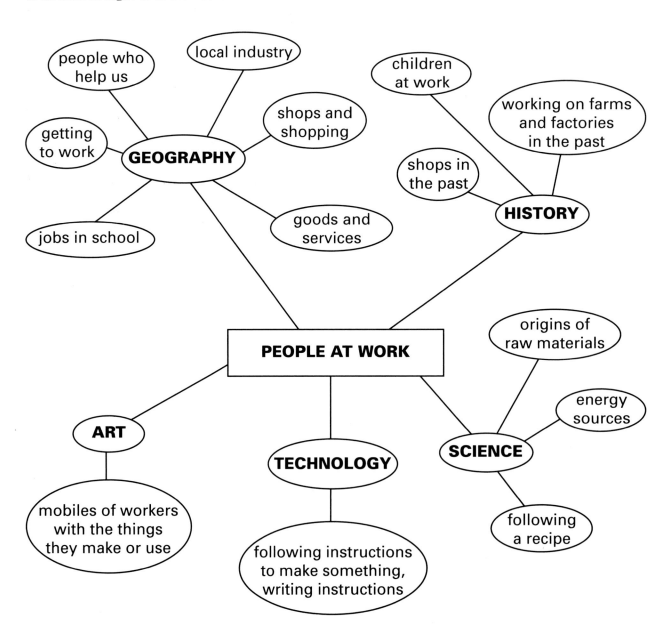

People at work – main Statements of Attainment

AT4 1c   Pupils should be able to recognise that adults do different kinds of work.
AT4 2c   Pupils should be able to identify how goods and services needed in the local community are provided.

Related activities

Attainment Target 2
Activity 2.9   School jobs
Activity 2.10 Job fact files
Activity 2.11 Tools and equipment
Activity 2.14 Street work
Activity 2.15 Mime a job

Attainment Target 4
Activity 4.6   Places of work
Activity 4.19 What is work?
Activity 4.20 Everyday jobs
Activity 4.21 People who help us
Activity 4.22 A place of work
Activity 4.23 Car production line
Activity 4.24 Acting a job
Activity 4.25 A dictionary of jobs
Activity 4.26 Jobs around the world
Activity 4.27 Job detective

Activity 4.28 Music while you work
Activity 4.44 Journeys for work
Activity 4.49 Goods
Activity 4.50 Emergency services
Activity 4.51 Services in school
Activity 4.52 Role play
Activity 4.53 Race games
Activity 4.54 Shopping street
Activity 4.55 Adopt a shop
Activity 4.56 Markets
Activity 4.57 Networks
Activity 4.58 Local goods and services
Activity 4.59 Goods and services overseas

Attainment Target 5
Activity 5.25 Farming, fishing and mining
Activity 5.30 Deliveries
Activity 5.52 Working for the environment

VILLAGES AND TOWNS

For well over a century the majority of people in the United Kingdom have lived in towns and cities. Recently, improvements in communication and energy distribution have encouraged city dwellers to move back to the countryside. This process has broken down the clear distinction between towns and villages. There are now a substantial number of people who live in rural areas but who do not depend on the land for their livelihood.

The study of settlements is of central concern to geographers, and this blurring of traditional boundaries is of great interest to them. The idea is far too complex for young children to consider. However, they need to acquire the basic concepts of 'village', 'town' and 'city' so that they have yardsticks by which to measure more subtle distinctions as they get older.

There are many stories which emphasise the difference between town and country and which point up contrasts in lifestyles. The traditional village buildings – church, inn, shop and houses – are often described in detail. These are compared with the more opulent city streets. As well as finding out about historical settlements, children can investigate their own local area and consider its key features. Outdoor work and first-hand observations have an important part to play in this.

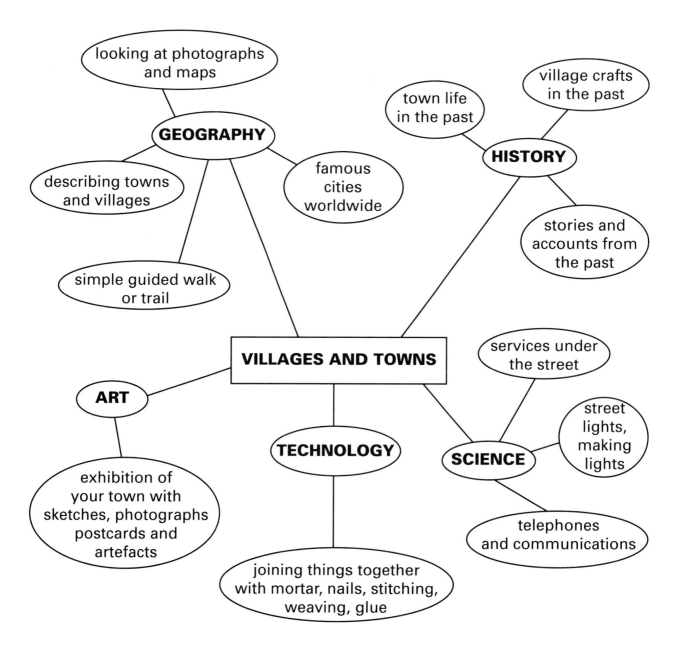

Villages and towns – main Statement of Attainment

AT4 2a Pupils should be able to demonstrate an understanding that most homes are part of a settlement, and that settlements vary in size.

Related activities

Attainment Target 1
Activity 1.26 Jigsaw scenes
Activity 1.65 Picture viewer

Attainment Target 2
Activity 2.5   Places alphabet
Activity 2.47 Capital cities
Activity 2.68 Village visit
Activity 2.69 Fishing port
Activity 2.70 Mining community
Activity 2.71 Tourist attraction

Attainment Target 4
Activity 4.29 Street survey
Activity 4.30 Where we live
Activity 4.31 Types of houses
Activity 4.32 Making a settlement
Activity 4.33 Wall map
Activity 4.34 Photograph album
Activity 4.35 Town model
Activity 4.36 Newspaper city
Activity 4.37 Paint a story
Activity 4.38 Concertina book

OTHER LANDS

Before the advent of the National Curriculum, children in infant schools were rarely taught about other parts of the world. Now all children have to learn about distant places. The web diagram shows how it is possible to create an integrated topic around this theme.

From a geographical point of view, it is important to concentrate on key ideas. Look at daily family life in the place you have chosen. Consider food, clothing, homes, work and other activities. How are services provided? What are the natural resources? How does the weather influence people? This approach will highlight geographical features and avoid the danger of creating a picturesque 'travelogue'.

These different enquiries will require a range of secondary sources such as books, artefacts, filmstrips and video films. Other subject areas may be used to enlarge the topic. Stories of exploration will add a historical dimension. A survey of machines and equipment from other countries provides a link to the science curriculum. You could also get the children to make a box or 'time capsule' to convey an impression of everyday life in the United Kingdom. This will illustrate the importance of modern technology and show how life in the United Kingdom differs from life in previous times and from life in other parts of the world.

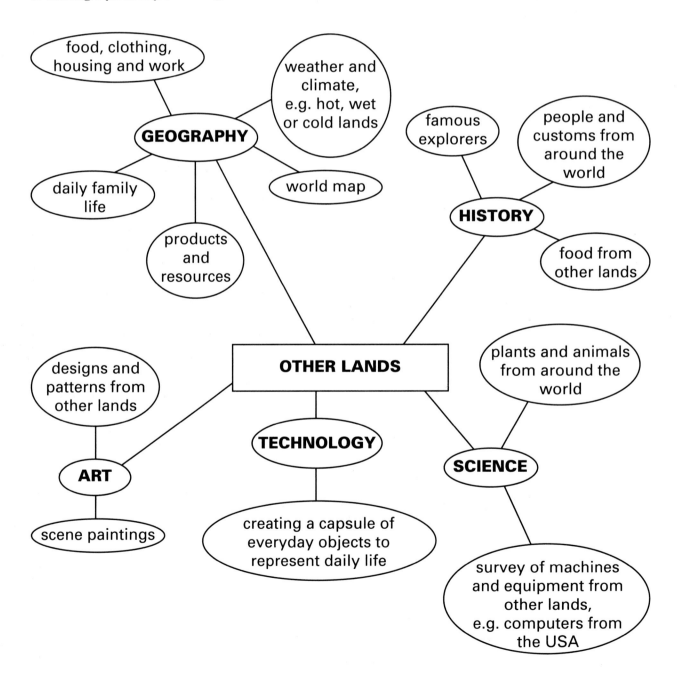

Other lands – main Statements of Attainment

AT2 1d Pupils should be able to demonstrate an awareness of the world beyond their local area.
AT2 2a Pupils should be able to name the countries of the United Kingdom.
AT2 2d Pupils should be able to describe similarities and differences between the local area and another locality specified in the programme of study.

Related activities

Attainment Target 1
Activity 1.15 North and South Pole
Activity 1.25 Looking at photographs
Activity 1.30 World map
Activity 1.39 Adventure story
Activity 1.40 Treasure island
Activity 1.59 World weather
Activity 1.62 Postcards
Activity 1.63 Other countries
Activity 1.64 Comparisons
Activity 1.66 Copying pictures
Activity 1.67 Library quiz

Attainment Target 2
Activity 2.28 Food
Activity 2.29 Clothes
Activity 2.30 House shapes
Activity 2.31 Holidays
Activity 2.32 Travellers
Activity 2.33 Soft toys
Activity 2.34 Different scenes
Activity 2.35 World museum
Activity 2.36 World music
Activity 2.37 Different languages
Activity 2.43 Borders
Activity 2.44 Imaginary map
Activity 2.45 World map
Activity 2.46 Stamps
Activity 2.47 Capital cities
Activity 2.48 The British Isles
Activity 2.49 Different countries

Activity 2.50 Countries snap
Activity 2.51 Different flags
Activity 2.52 The Union Jack
Activity 2.53 Connections
Activity 2.54 Impressions
Activity 2.55 Countries game
Activity 2.56 Twister
Activity 2.57 Voices
Activity 2.72 School link
Activity 2.73 Contrasting photographs
Activity 2.74 Matching descriptions
Activity 2.75 Looking at pictures
Activity 2.76 Symbols
Activity 2.77 Objects
Activity 2.78 Twinning
Activity 2.79 Overseas communities
Activity 2.80 Television programmes
Activity 2.81 Posters, packs and videos

Attainment Target 4
Activity 4.8   Buildings around the world
Activity 4.26 Jobs around the world
Activity 4.38 Concertina book
Activity 4.47 Postcard corner
Activity 4.48 Adventure journeys
Activity 4.59 Goods and services overseas

Attainment Target 5
Activity 5.13 Food from different places
Activity 5.23 A far-away place

THE COUNTRYSIDE

This topic reflects the growing interest in and concern for the environment, and has the advantage of combining several key areas of the National Curriculum. Geographers are particularly concerned with the shape and form of the land, and the way that people have exploited natural resources through mining, quarrying and farming.

These ideas can be amplified in scientific studies by considering how growing conditions affect farming, and by associating rock, soil and water with the landforms and the habitats that they produce. Changes in landscapes and living conditions provide a link with history, while art and technology can be introduced through design problems and through techniques of representing the natural world.

Rural schools may well be able to provide children with first-hand experiences. However, even in urban areas there will be opportunities for fieldwork. You can get the children to investigate a variety of different questions: Are the playground and school site flat? Where do building materials come from? How do we obtain our daily food? How do we dispose of rubbish and waste? What are the possibilities for recycling? This might lead to a practical outcome in which the children take part in their own conservation project.

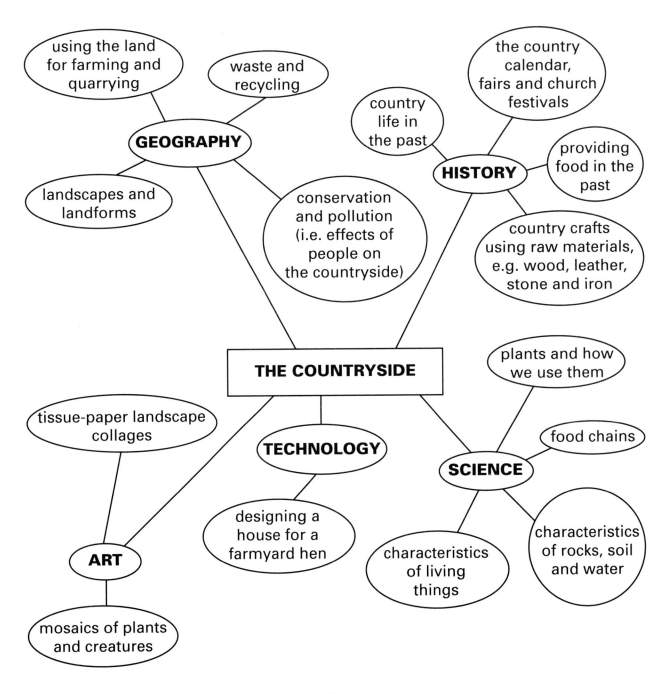

The countryside – main Statements of Attainment

AT5 1a Pupils should be able to identify and name materials obtained from natural resources.
AT5 2a Pupils should be able to identify how people obtain materials from the environment.
AT5 2b Pupils should be able to describe ways in which people have changed the environment.
AT5 2c Pupils should be able to suggest how they could improve the quality of their own environment.

Related activities

Attainment Target 1
Activity 1.3   Model farm
Activity 1.27 Landscapes
Activity 1.37 Scenes

Attainment Target 2
Activity 2.67 Farm visit

Attainment Target 3
Activity 3.1   Rock collection
Activity 3.2   Feely box
Activity 3.3   Miniature garden
Activity 3.4   Looking at sand
Activity 3.5   Different soils

Attainment Target 5
Activity 5.1   Natural resources
Activity 5.2   Associations
Activity 5.3   Resources in the classroom
Activity 5.4   Resources and products mobile
Activity 5.5   Wood rubbings
Activity 5.6   Woollen clothes
Activity 5.7   Miniature characters
Activity 5.8   Clothes shop
Activity 5.9   Made of iron

Activity 5.10 Zig-zag book
Activity 5.11 Paper making
Activity 5.12 Butter making
Activity 5.13 Food from different places
Activity 5.14 Animal, vegetable or mineral?
Activity 5.24 Raw materials
Activity 5.25 Farming, fishing and mining
Activity 5.26 Machines
Activity 5.27 Different sources
Activity 5.28 Quarry trail
Activity 5.29 How are they obtained?
Activity 5.30 Deliveries
Activity 5.31 Underground scene
Activity 5.32 Fishing fleet
Activity 5.33 Fish mobile
Activity 5.34 Change dial
Activity 5.35 Farms and factories
Activity 5.36 Change in your locality
Activity 5.37 Obsolete objects
Activity 5.38 New things
Activity 5.39 Door walk
Activity 5.40 Advertisements
Activity 5.41 Favourite building
Activity 5.42 Wear and tear

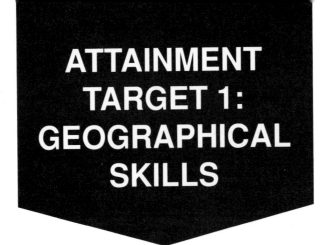

ATTAINMENT TARGET 1: GEOGRAPHICAL SKILLS

Pupils should demonstrate their ability to use skills to support work for the other Attainment Targets in geography, and in particular:

i) the use of maps; and
ii) fieldwork techniques.

Programme of Study for Key Stage 1 (Levels 1 & 2 only. For Level 3 see p. 50)

Geographical skills

1 Enquiry should form an important part of pupils' work in geography in Key Stage 1. Work should be linked to pupils' own interests, experience and capabilities and should lead to investigations based on both fieldwork and classroom activities. Much of pupils' learning in Key Stage 1 should be based on direct experience, practical activities and exploration of the local area.

2 Pupils should be encouraged to ask geographical questions, *for example, 'Why is this place like it is?',* and to search for answers with the guidance of their teachers. Pupils should be given opportunities to use information technology (IT). They should be taught to:

- observe their surroundings, and examine pictures and pictorial maps of distant places, and use an increasing range of geographical terms, *for example, hill, slope, river, road, house, shop,* in describing what they see;

- identify similarities and differences between places, *for example, in the ways land and buildings are used and in the life and work of people;*

- select information that is relevant to a geographical study from material provided by the teacher, *for example, select pictures of lakes, rivers and seas for a study of water.*

3 Pupils should be taught to:

- follow directions, including the terms forwards and backwards, up and down, left and right, north, south, east and west;

- extract information from, and add it to, pictorial maps;

- draw around object to make a plan, *for example, mathematical shapes and household objects;*

- make representations of actual or imaginary places, *for example, their own bedroom, a treasure island;*

- identify land and sea on maps and globes;

- follow a route on a map, *for example, a map of the local area of the school produced by a teacher, another adult or a pupil;*

- use pictures and photographs to identify features, *for example, homes, railways, rivers, hills,* and to find out about places;

- observe, describe and record the weather over a short period.

ABOUT THIS ATTAINMENT TARGET ▷

Geographers seek to describe the world. In order to do this they have pioneered a number of special skills and techniques. Fieldwork enables geographers to collect information and data about conditions in different places. Maps are one way in which this information can be analysed and presented. No other subject makes such extensive use of maps and fieldwork. This Attainment Target highlights these distinctive geographical skills.

In teaching children mapwork it is best to begin with large-scale maps of the local area. Children should also use maps in context. The classroom, school building and grounds provide a safe and familiar environment in which they can practise basic skills. Globes and world maps can be introduced as occasion permits to enhance the children's knowledge of distant places.

All geographical work done outside the classroom is known as fieldwork. With infants the main focus will be on sensory perception, vocabulary and data collection. If children are to have a chance to develop skills in these areas they will need to undertake fieldwork on a regular basis. Over a period of time this will enable them to build up an increasingly sophisticated image of their immediate surroundings.

As they conduct their studies, children should be encouraged to ask questions. Just as historians use evidence to find out about the past, so geographers depend on enquiries and investigations. Practical work has an important part to play in geography, and can contribute greatly to the enjoyment and appreciation of the subject.

Geographical skills have strong links with other areas of the curriculum. Map-reading skills, for example, are useful in gathering information about the past. Maps can indicate changes in settlement patterns. They also involve mathematics through use of coordinates, scales and measurements. Equally, fieldwork observations need to be analysed and presented. English, mathematics, art, technology and science all have a part to play.

BACKGROUND INFORMATION FOR THE TEACHER ▷

The use of maps

All maps interpret the world selectively. Political maps, for example, show the boundaries between countries. A mariner's chart, by contrast, provides information about ocean currents and the depth of the sea bed. Today, almost any kind of information can be presented in map form. Maps are increasingly being used to provide information on environmental and social issues such as population growth, pollution and deforestation.

The problem facing all map-makers is how to represent the earth, which is three-dimensional, on a two-dimensional piece of paper. The solution lies in the use of mathematical grids or projections. One of the most famous projections was devised by Mercator in the sixteenth century to guide the exploration of the earth. In recent times Arno Peters has popularised a projection which, unlike Mercator's, shows areas more accurately. This has been favoured by many aid agencies as it challenges Eurocentric perceptions.

Fieldwork techniques

Geographers have a long tradition of visiting different places and experiencing them directly. Just as scientists do not theorise about the behaviour of matter until they have conducted tests and experiments, so geographers need to collect information at first hand before they can analyse it. Trails, surveys, questionnaires and maps are all used. Specialist equipment such as tape measures, compasses and thermometers provide more specific data.

Map projections

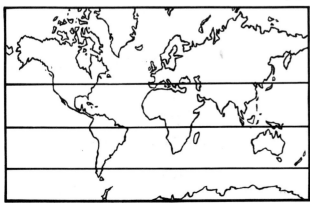

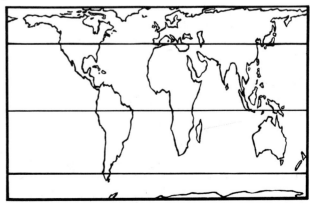

Mercator's projection shows direction accurately but enlarges the polar regions.

Peter's projection shows area accurately but distorts the shape of the continents.

Facts and figures
- The oldest surviving map of the world was made by the Babylonians, and is carved on a clay tablet.

- The Greeks were the first to deduce that the earth is a sphere.

- Maps were crucial to the exploration of the world in the sixteenth century.

- The Ordnance Survey organisation began to map the UK in 1791 and took until 1902 to finish.

- Modern computer-generated maps show the world in three dimensions and allow the viewer to zoom in on particular areas and to change their position.

 Area of Study 1 # FOLLOW DIRECTIONS CM 1.1 –1.4

Statement of Attainment

Level **1**

1a) Pupils should be able to follow directions.

Example and links with the Programme of Study
Pupils should be able to follow directions round the classroom, the school building and the school site. They should be able to use the terms forwards and backwards, up and down, left and right, north, south, east and west in practical situations.

Introduction
One of the first skills that very young children learn is how to cope with their immediate physical surroundings. They become aware of the location of objects within the first few months of their lives. As they grow older, children come to realise that the external world has a permanent existence.

Young children are highly egocentric and define the position of objects in relation to themselves. For example, a baby girl lying in her cot may have her teddy in front of her and her rattle above her. When she stands up and turns round this spatial relationship alters. As they grow older, infants still find spatial awareness a problem because they use a wider range of directional vocabulary and they move in more complex surroundings.

The Statement of Attainment requires children to follow directions, which means they must apply their knowledge. It also implies that they are able to follow instructions. This is one of the requirements of the English curriculum. There is a range of specific vocabulary which children will need to use if they are to cope with these demands.

Key vocabulary

above	forwards
backwards	in front
behind	left
below	near
compass	north
direction	right
down	south
east	up
far	west

Key questions
Who follows directions?
Have you ever given directions?
What things show directions?
What happens to people when they lose their sense of direction?

Picture books
The Journey Home by Joanne Plindall (Walker, 1988) is ideal for supporting work on this Statement of Attainment. Each double-page spread shows a family driving home through a landscape. There are plenty of things to talk about and discuss with the children.

Rhymes

The Grand Old Duke of York

Oh, the Grand Old Duke of York,
He had ten thousand men;
He marched them up to the top of the hill,
And he marched them down again.

Now when they were up, they were up;
And when they were down, they were down;
But when they were only half-way up,
They were neither up nor down.

Mr East gave a Feast

Mr East gave a feast,
Mr North laid the cloth,
Mr West did his best,
Mr South burnt his mouth
With eating a cold potato.

Songs
'The Bear went over the Mountain', from *Apusskidu* by Beatrice Harrop (Black, 1975) is appropriate.

Activity 1.1: Direction words

Working from the key vocabulary list, decide which directional words the children need to learn. Use these words in as many practical situations as possible. You could get the children to follow directions when they want to find things in class, when you are playing games in the hall, or to point things out on an environmental walk. Reinforce the work by playing a game of 'Simon Says'. Are there any direction words which make interesting clapping patterns in time to music?

Activity 1.2: Blindfold donkey game

Materials needed
Scarf or other material to make a blindfold and 'tail'.

Play the blindfold donkey game either with groups of children or with the whole class. You will need to select one child to be the donkey. The child is then blindfolded and given a tail. Other children call out directions for the donkey to follow. These should specify the number of paces as well as the direction. The challenge is for the child to follow the instructions correctly. You can play the game as a time-filler when you have a few minutes to spare at the end of a lesson. As the children get more experienced, you can make the instructions more complicated.

Activity 1.3: Model farm

Materials needed
Toy farm buildings and animals, instruction cards.

Make some instruction cards for the children to use when they play with toy buildings and animals. The instructions should use directional words, and help the children to construct a model of a farm. You might ask them to put the cat in front of the shed, or the horse in the field. When the children are familiar with the layout you can change the instructions. You could also ask them to bring some toys of their own to add to the scene.

Activity 1.4: Arrows

Materials needed
Light card, scissors.

Play some direction games using arrows. Cut these out from light card. Get the children to lay the arrows on the floor to show the way to the sink, home corner, library corner or other points of interest. Ask the children to describe the routes they have made up. Now remove the arrows and see if a child can reach the correct destination by following the instructions only.

Activity 1.5: Left and right

Materials needed
Ribbons of different colours, crayons, paper.

Give the children ribbons to tie on to their wrists. They should have two different colours, one for the left and the other for the right. Get them to make a drawing showing things to the left and right of where they sit. They can colour the things to match the colour of their ribbons and write the words left and right in large letters at the top of their drawings.

Activity 1.6: Left and right stick

Materials needed
Some light sticks, scissors, card, Sellotape.

Get the children to draw round their hands on a piece of card. They should then label the shapes 'left' and 'right', cut them out and fix them to the end of a light stick using Sellotape. Working in pairs, the children can now go on short journeys with their sticks. One of the children should call out directions, such as 'Turn right', while the other, who holds the stick, obeys them like a robot. After a while the children should swap places so they both get a turn at following instructions.

Activity 1.7: Left and right survey

Do a survey on left and right by looking at things in the classroom. How many pieces of furniture have catches or handles on the left? How many have them on the right? How many children are left-handed? When you go on a classroom journey, how many times do you turn left and right? **Copymaster 1.1** (Left and Right Survey) has been designed to help children record their answers. You might also make a class display of the findings in the form of a table and pictures.

6 children write with their left hand.

20 children write with their right hand.

HANDS

left	6
right	20

Direction finder. Make a direction finder by fixing the arrow to the cardboard circle with a paper fastener.

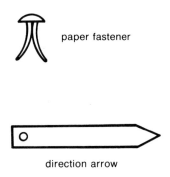

paper fastener

direction arrow

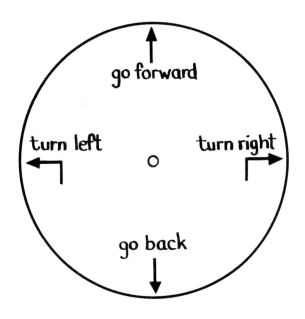

Activity 1.8: Direction finder

Materials needed

Light card, paper fasteners, scissors.

Get the children to make a simple direction finder. They will need to cut out a circle about 10 cm in diameter from light card. They should then write the words 'go forward', 'go back', 'turn left', 'turn right' at the correct points and fix an arrow to the centre with a paper fastener. By turning the arrow the children will be able to give themselves instructions and create routes round the classroom. The direction finder will encourage them to make 90° turns. It will also help to reinforce the idea of left and right.

Activity 1.9: Mystery trail

Materials needed

Direction finders (see activity 1.8), light card, dice.

Make up some routes for the children to follow using their direction finders. You could write down the instructions on pieces of card. Where does each route lead to? Are there any obstacles that get in the way? You could extend the activity by letting the children fill in the number of steps that they are going to take in each direction by throwing a dice.

Activity 1.10: Programmable toy

Materials needed

Programmable toy or robot (e.g. Big Trak, Turtle, Roamer), computer, computer program.

Set up a programmable toy or robot which the children can play with in groups. When they have got used to the equipment you can ask them to work out a program for it to follow. This might involve going forwards, backwards, left and right. Enter the program into the computer and see if it works in practice. What other programs can the children devise for the toy to follow?

A programmable toy and computer

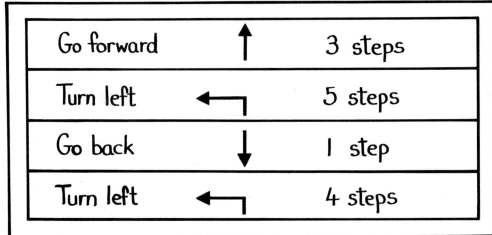

Go forward	↑	3 steps
Turn left	←	5 steps
Go back	↓	1 step
Turn left	←	4 steps

Instructions for a mystery trail

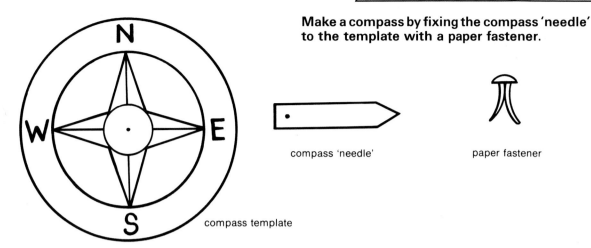

Make a compass by fixing the compass 'needle' to the template with a paper fastener.

compass 'needle'

paper fastener

compass template

Activity 1.11: Signs in school

Materials needed
Card, artwork materials.

Look round your school to see if you can discover any arrows or direction signs. What do they tell you? Are they easy to follow? Discuss any signs which it might be useful to have either in your school or class. Make them out of card and fix them to suitable places. You might have signs pointing to the book corner, sink, places to put rubbish, and so on.

Activity 1.12: Signs in the street

Take the children on a walk in the streets near your school to see how traffic signs are used. How many can they find? What do they tell us? Discuss each one in turn. You could get the children to record their findings in drawings, or give them **Copymaster 1.2** (Street Signs) to complete. Find out more about traffic signs when you return to school. *The Highway Code* is one of the best reference sources. You could either use this directly or make up a reference sheet illustrating a few important signs.

Activity 1.13: Compass directions

Materials needed
Compass, sugar paper.

Using a compass, find out which way is north, south, east and west from your classroom. Write large direction labels on some sheets of sugar paper and pin them to the correct walls. Talk about the different compass directions with the children. What can they see to the north of them? What can they see to the south? Repeat this exercise in the hall or playground. You could ask the children to record their findings either in words or pictures, using **Copymaster 1.3** (Compass Directions). Extend the work in direction and movement games. Can the children touch the north wall, point to the east wall, and so on?

Activity 1.14: Make a compass

Materials needed
Card, scissors, crayons, paper fasteners, compass.

Get the children to make their own compass. They could either colour and cut out the compass in **Copymaster 1.4** (Compass Model), or you could provide them with a compass cut-out of your own. When they have cut out the compass shape they should add a 'needle' by fixing an arrow to the middle of the compass with a paper fastener. The children can align their models with a real compass at different points around the school. This will reinforce the idea of the different directions and help them to understand how a real compass is used.

Activity 1.15: North and South Pole

Materials needed
Globe or world map.

Talk to the children about where you would get to if you kept on travelling north. Do they have any ideas? Look at a globe or world map to find the arctic and lands of the north. Explain that the earth is a sphere which spins in space. Which two places stay stationary? What are they called? What are the differences between the North and South Poles?

Copymasters

1.1 Left and Right Survey Children can either draw or name all the things which they find on the left and right in this survey sheet.

1.2 Street Signs This copymaster is designed to be used on an environmental walk. The children tick the different things as they discover them.

1.3 Compass Directions You could use this copymaster either in the classroom or out-of-doors to help the children record what they can see to the north and south.

1.4 Compass Model This sheet provides an outline for a compass model. The children should colour the pieces before they cut them out. The copymaster is best reproduced on light card if possible.

TALK ABOUT A FAMILIAR PLACE

CM 1.5 –1.6

| Area of Study 2 |

Statement of Attainment

Level 1

1b) Pupils should be able to observe and talk about a familiar place.

Example and links with the Programme of Study

Children should talk about their immediate surroundings and consider physical, human and environmental aspects of their home, school and neighbourhood.

Introduction

Geographers study and describe different places around the world. The National Curriculum requires that young children describe places too. This Statement of Attainment focuses attention on the places that children know best – their home and school. More mature children may also be able to look more widely at the local area.

When they make their observations, the children will be using rudimentary enquiry skills. It is important that they are encouraged to think geographically, sorting what they see into categories such as houses and shops, and describing things using specific vocabulary. In later years their knowledge and understanding of the local area will serve as a basis from which they can make comparisons with the wider world.

Key vocabulary

buildings	railway
church	river
classroom	road
country	school
factory	shop
farm	slope
field	station
forest	street
hill	town
house	train
lake	trees
park	village

Key questions

What are the main landscape features where you live?
What are the main buildings?
What are the main methods of transport?
Is the environment attractive?

Rhymes

This Little Puffin by Elizabeth Matterson (Penguin, 1969) has a section of poems and rhymes called 'In the House' which relates directly to this Statement of Attainment.

Here is a House

Here is a house built up high,
(Stretch arms up, touching fingertips)
With two tall chimneys reaching the sky.
(Stretch arms up separately)
Here are the windows,
(Make square shape with hands)
Here is the door.
(Knock)
If we peep inside, we'll see a mouse on the floor.
(Raise hands in fright)

Songs

The children may enjoy 'Tipsy Topsy Turvy Town' from *The Music Box Songbook* (BBC, 1987) as it is full of simple absurdities.

Activity 1.16: Our school

Materials needed

Large sheets of paper and artwork materials.

Talk with the class about the school. How many classrooms are there? How many teachers? What are the walls made of? How many different entrances are there? Is the building all on the same floor or level? Ask the children to make paintings of the school, showing the things which they think are important. Put these up as a class display and add notes highlighting the main features shown.

Activity 1.17: School photo quiz

Materials needed

Camera and film.

Take some photographs of different features of the school building such as doors, windows and decorations. Give the photographs to a group of children and see if they can find the things shown. You might need to sort the photographs into groups or give the children clues as to where to search if they get stuck. When the children have finished the quiz you could ask them to make pencil drawings of the things shown in the pictures and mount them with captions as a wall display.

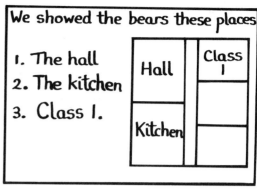

Activity 1.18: Teddy bear visit

Materials needed

Teddy Bears, camera and film, scrapbook.

Arrange for the children to bring their teddy bears to school for the day. (Make sure that bears are provided for any children who don't have their own bear.) Talk with the children about the places and things they should show their bears. Where can they play? Where can they go for a drink? Where do they work? Take photographs of the bears in these different places and mount them in a book called 'Teddy Comes to School'. The children should write a sentence under each photograph. With more mature children you might also include a simple map at the beginning showing the places visited.

Activity 1.19: Classroom windows

Materials needed

Fabric, coloured paper and other materials for a collage.

Discuss with the children what they can see through one of the classroom windows. Can they identify houses, trees, churches, shops, fields, hedges, hills, clouds, and so on? Put out some fabric, coloured paper and other materials and ask the children to make a collage of the view. Mount the collages on the wall and

add labels naming the key features. Use **Copymaster 1.5** (Window View) as a way of extending the work.

Activity 1.20: Different views

Compare the view from four or five different windows around the school. Which window has the most interesting view? From which window can you see most things? Which window has your favourite view? Get the children to vote on the view they like most. Make up some sentences to record the children's opinions, for example, 'Seven children like the view from the hall window', 'You can see five different buildings from the windows in Class 1'.

Activity 1.21: Streets and houses

Materials needed

Crayons, small sheets of paper, a map of your locality.

Ask the children to make a drawing of their home using pencil and crayons. Remind them to show the key features, such as the doors, windows, roof and chimney. Mount the pictures in the form of a map and add the names of local streets. See if the children can bring photographs of their homes to school to mount alongside their drawings. Collect further information using **Copymaster 1.6** (My Home).

Pin labels to the features in a landscape scene.

35

Activity 1.22: Our locality

Materials needed
Large-scale map of the locality, computer and database program.

Working as a class or in groups, discuss all the different places and buildings you can think of in your locality. You may find it helpful to look at a large-scale map of the locality. Make a list of facts and figures. How many churches are there? How many shops? How many streets? Is there a park? If possible, enter these facts and figures into a simple computer database and print out the statistics.

Copymasters

1.5 Window View   This sheet focuses on the physical environment. Children should colour the scene as well as completing the labels from the words at the bottom.

1.6 My Home   Children will need to take this sheet home to answer the questions. A parent or older brother or sister could help them if necessary.

USE GEOGRAPHICAL VOCABULARY

Area of Study 3

CM 1.7 –1.10

Statement of Attainment

Level **2**

2a) Pupils should be able to use geographical vocabulary to talk about places.

Example and links with the Programme of Study
Children should talk about features of their immediate environment, discuss different types of map, and develop their knowledge and understanding of distant places.

Introduction
The relationship between thought and language is highly complex. However, it seems that unless children have appropriate vocabulary, they will be unable to develop their ideas. This Statement of Attainment draws attention to the role of language in promoting learning.

Like any subject, geography has its own specialist terminology. At infant level many of these terms are part of everyday speech. This reflects the fact that geographers describe the world around us. When identifying the words that young children need to know it is often helpful to think in terms of categories or groups. For this reason the list of key vocabulary below is sorted into groups.

When teaching this Statement of Attainment you need to remember that children need a lot of practice in using new vocabulary before they fully understand its use. Children often guess what to do when the whole class is given instructions, and it only becomes clear that they have not understood what to do when they are asked to work on their own. Constant reinforcement of what is being taught and the opportunity to use vocabulary in different ways will help children to develop their ability to recall the vocabulary.

Key vocabulary
Spatial

backwards	below	far
behind	down	forwards
left	right	
near	up	

Routes

alley	railway	subway
bypass	road	track
footpath	route	
motorway	street	

Landscape

bank	mountain	stream
cliff	river	wood
field	sea	
hill	slope	

Boundaries

barrier	fence	shore
boundary	gate	wall
bridge	hedge	
edge	kerb	

Settlements

buildings	hotel	shop
church	house	supermarket
factory	office	
garage	school	

Key questions
What words describe our position or location?
What words describe the landscape?
What words describe buildings and places?
What words describe routes?
What words describe boundaries?

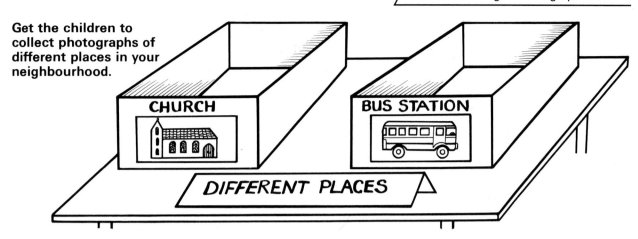

Get the children to collect photographs of different places in your neighbourhood.

CHURCH   BUS STATION

DIFFERENT PLACES

Picture books

Many picture books use geographical vocabulary as a natural part of the story. *We're Going on a Bear Hunt* by Michael Rosen and Helen Oxenbury (Walker, 1989) is a good example. The search in the story leads to lots of different places including a cave and a forest. *Anno's Journey* by Mitsumasa Anno (Bodley, 1977) adopts a different format but also helps to stimulate vocabulary. It is a picture book without words that takes the reader on a journey across the landscapes of Europe.

Activity 1.23: The neighbourhood

Materials needed
Old shoe boxes or cardboard boxes.

Talk with the children about the school and its neighbourhood. What different buildings are there? What routes do people use? Are there any special places, such as a park or old castle? Choose three or four key places and get the children to bring items from them to school for display. For example, they might bring old tickets, pictures, timetables and brochures from the bus station. Make a box for each place. You could put labels and photographs on the front and set them up as a small exhibition.

Activity 1.24: Personal feelings

Materials needed
Large-scale plan of the school.

Make a collection of words which describe what we feel about different places. Examples could include 'interesting', 'quiet', 'noisy', 'exciting', 'colourful', 'frightening', and so on. Visit some places around the

school and get the children to say which words best describe their feelings. When they return to the class ask the children to write some simple sentences about what they felt. You could pin these to a large-scale map of the school to make a wall display. Are there any places which some children like but which others dislike? Which places do the children generally like to visit?

Activity 1.25: Looking at photographs

Materials needed
Photographs of scenes from around the world.

Give the children some pictures to look at showing scenes from around the world. Discuss what they show. Get the children to select two which they find particularly interesting and to record information about them using **Copymaster 1.7** (Looking at Photographs). Extend the work by showing the class some slides of different places. What are the key features in each picture? Can the children guess the country or continent?

Activity 1.26: Jigsaw scenes

Materials needed
A selection of simple jigsaws.

Give the children some simple jigsaws to complete, showing town or country scenes. Talk with them about the different things in the picture. Ask them to make a list of appropriate words using geographical headings such as 'buildings', 'transport' or 'scenery'. You could extend the work by giving the class **Copymaster 1.8** (Jigsaw). The children should colour the picture and talk about the different features they can see. They could then cut up the pieces and try to put them together in the correct order. Alternatively, you could play a game of beetle, in which the children throw a dice to see which pieces they collect. The winner is the first person to make up a complete scene.

Activity 1.27: Landscapes

Materials needed
Frieze paper, scissors, glue.

I like the playground because it is noisy.
John

Ask the children to colour **Copymaster 1.9** (Landscapes), and cut out the pictures. They should then try to arrange them in a logical order, from the peak to the sea. Check that the children have put the pictures in a sensible sequence and get them to glue them down on a piece of frieze paper. Finally, display the work on the classroom wall and discuss any differences that you notice. Although there is an overall pattern, the children may have decided to put the wood and field in a variety of different positions.

Activity 1.28: Word scales

Get the children to make a list of all the words they can think of which describe different types of wind. Put them down in random order and then try to sort them into a sequence. For example, you might start with 'calm' and 'light breeze' at one end of the scale and conclude with 'gale' and 'hurricane' at the other. Ask the children to make drawings to go with some of the words. Put them up with captions as a class display.

CALM
Smoke rises upwards

BREEZE
Kites fly

WINDY
Waves at sea

GALE
Trees blow over

Think about some other word scales. For example, there are lots of different words that describe temperature, or settlements (hamlets, villages, towns and so on), or types of transport.

Activity 1.29: Picture maps

Materials needed
Picture and tourist maps.

Look at some picture or tourist maps of your own area. What are the features which are shown? Ask the children to make their own drawings for a class wall map. Get them to add labels or descriptions. Can the children think of any other features they would like to add? Look at picture maps of other places in other parts of the country. What do these tell you about the places? Would you like to go there?

Activity 1.30: World map

Materials needed
World map or globe.

Look at a world map or globe. Discuss what it shows. Can the children find the British Isles? What colours are used for the land and sea? Where are the North and South Poles? Why are they special? What is the name of the imaginary line (equator) which goes round the middle of the earth? Why is it important?

Copymasters

1.7 Looking At Photographs This copymaster will help children use geographical vocabulary to record information from photographs. They should tick one box for each pair of words and write a short descriptive sentence for each picture.

1.8 Jigsaw The children should colour the picture and cut the copymaster into six pieces. They can then either try to reassemble the picture or collect the pieces by throwing a dice, as in a game of beetle.

1.9 Landscapes The children should colour the pictures, cut them out, and arrange them in a logical sequence to make a frieze.

1.10 World Map The children should colour the sea and land using crayons or felt tips and identify the position of the British Isles.

Area of Study 4 — **REPRESENT PLACES ON A MAP** CM 1.11 –1.14

Level 2	**Statement of Attainment**
	2b) Pupils should be able to make a representation of a real or an imaginary place.

Example and links with the Programme of Study
The children should draw round everyday objects to make simple plans, they should make maps or pictures of their classroom and other familiar environments, and represent imaginary places such as a treasure island.

Introduction

Mapwork is the most distinctive geographical skill. The ability to make a permanent visual record of the environment is one of the most significant human achievements. It has enabled people to record journeys and voyages, identify their location and communicate information about distant places. Maps have played a key role in the development of knowledge, and must rank alongside the invention of the wheel in allowing people to break out of their immediate surroundings, conquer distance and dominate the planet.

There are two main types of map. Conventional maps portray the world according to a number of agreed rules which include the use of symbols, scale and orientation. Conceptual maps, on the other hand, are much more personal. These are the maps we carry in our heads and which enable us to find our way from one place to another.

This Statement of Attainment focuses on conceptual mapping. It encourages children to draw their own plans or pictures of different places, both familiar and unfamiliar. These should indicate spatial relationships, but need not follow set rules. The children will be fascinated by the problem of representing three-dimensional reality on a two-dimensional piece of paper.

Key vocabulary

above	landmark	scale
code	map	shape
direction	north	sign
grid	plan	symbol
key	route	way

Key questions

What things are shown on maps and plans?
What is the difference between a picture and a plan?
What different types of maps are there?
Who uses maps and plans?

Legends

The race between the hare and the tortoise in Aesop's *Fables* appeals to children and captures their imagination. You might ask them to make a drawing or picture map of the route.

Picture books

Some picture books describe routes and landmarks. *Rosie's Walk* by Pat Hutchins (Bodley, 1968) is one of the most well-known. *Spot's First Walk* by Eric Hill (Heinemann, 1981) is another suitable book. Adventure stories can provide more open-ended opportunities. *The Baron on the Island of Cheese* by Adrian Mitchell (Walker, 1986) is one of a series of tales which involve journeys around the world. These appeal to older children.

Activity 1.31: Overhead projector

Materials needed

Toy vehicles, models and other small objects, overhead projector, paper.

Collect together a number of different objects that have interesting plans. Small toys and everyday objects are ideal. Place them, one at a time, on an overhead projector and shine the image on to the wall. Can the children guess the object from its plan? Why are plans always drawn from directly overhead? Pin some paper on the wall and get the children to draw round the shapes and cut them out for a class display. Are the children still able to recognise the different plans? Get them to write labels before they forget what the plans are of.

Activity 1.32: Plan views

Materials needed

A selection of everyday items, camera and film.

Take photographs of some everyday objects such as a saucepan, cup, table lamp and iron. You will need to take two photographs of each thing: one to show the side view (elevation), and the other to show the overhead view (plan). If possible, mount the photographs on card and cover them for protection. Talk with the children about what they can see in each photograph. Does it show the view from above, or a side view? Can they sort the photographs into sets and match them with the objects? Ask them to draw the plan view for themselves. Use **Copymaster 1.11** (Plan Views) to develop the work.

Activity 1.33: Tray game

Materials needed

A number of objects and labels, tray, light card, scissors.

Place a number of objects on a tray. Ask the children to make a plan of each one by drawing round the outline

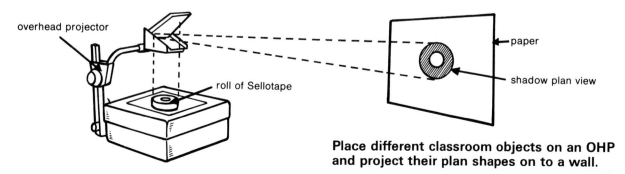

Place different classroom objects on an OHP and project their plan shapes on to a wall.

Tray game. See if the children can match the objects on a tray with their plan shape.

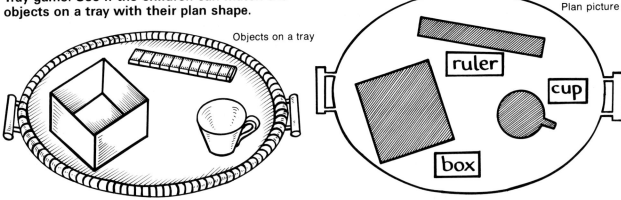

Objects on a tray

Plan picture

on to a piece of card. Get them to cut out the shapes. See if they can make plans which match the objects on the tray. When you have checked that they are correct, the children should add labels saying what each shape represents. You can repeat the game on a number of different occasions, adding more objects each time so that it becomes more complicated.

Activity 1.34: Class plan

Materials needed

Large class plan, small pieces of card.

Make a large class plan for a wall display. Talk about it with the children. Can they identify the windows, door, teacher's table, and so on? Ask them to write their name on a piece of card and pin it to the correct place on the plan to show where they sit. Add other labels to indicate the activity areas, for example the art corner and book corner. When the children are familiar with the plan you could use it for some class games. Move the names around before the children come into school and get them to work out where they must go and sit. Alternatively, you could ask all the children in the class to sit in different places. The children then have to make the plan match up with their new positions.

Activity 1.35: Signpost map

Materials needed

Classroom plans.

Either ask the children to draw a simple plan of the classroom, or duplicate one for them to use. Get them to put a cross to mark where they are sitting. They should then draw arrows to key points in the classroom such as the windows, door, teacher's desk and sink, and label them. Not only will this help the children to orientate themselves, it also gives them further experience in using a class plan.

Activity 1.36: Journey plan

Materials needed

Paper, crayons, felt tips, plasticine.

Ask the children to make a plan or picture of their journey to school. This should show the things that they pass, any important road crossings, and sharp turns or changes in direction. It is important to talk with the children about what they are going to show before they begin the work, but equally they need to be given a free hand and not constrained in how they choose to represent the route. Encourage them to add details to their plans as they remember things that

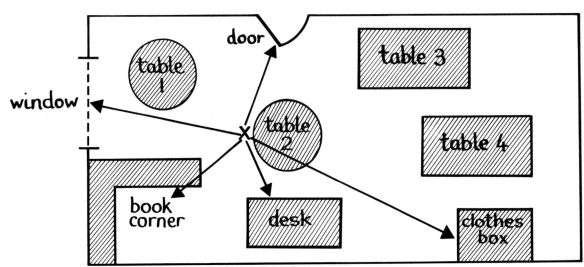

Signpost map. Ask the children to draw arrows from the place where they sit to different parts of the room.

they have left out. You might extend the exercise by asking the children to make a simple plasticine model based on their plans. You could follow up this work with **Copymaster 1.12** (Route Maze).

Activity 1.37: Scenes

Materials needed
Play mats, toy vehicles, farm animals, Lego.

Make or buy a series of play mats showing road patterns, farm layouts, and so on. Get the children to devise scenes using the mats as a base, and the toys from the play cupboard. When they are satisfied with a scene, ask the children to record the layout as a plan or picture on a piece of paper. Pack the materials away and see if the children can replace the pieces exactly as they were before, working from their drawings. As a variation, you could provide the children with plans that they have to follow as accurately as they can. **Copymaster 1.13** (Farm Scene) provides a linked extension exercise.

Activity 1.38: Adventure playground

Materials needed
Paper, crayons, scissors, glue.

Discuss with the children what equipment they would like to find in an adventure playground. They might suggest trampolines, assault courses, climbing frames, creatures to play on, a sandpit, ropes or swings. Ask them to do drawings of these different things, cut them out and arrange them on a plan. Discuss how they might be best positioned. How could the playground be made safe? Will there be somewhere for toddlers to play, as well as an area for older children? **Copymaster 1.14** (Adventure Playground) provides some drawings which children can colour and add to their plans if they run out of ideas.

Activity 1.39: Adventure story

Get the children to make up an adventure story about a journey or voyage at sea. What happens? What different places do they visit? Are there disasters or dangers they have to face? Ask the children to show

their story as a map or picture. They might make a sequence of linked drawings, or a unified scene in which all the different things take place. They should add notes round the edge explaining the details.

Activity 1.40: Treasure islands

Materials needed
Drawing paper, crayons, paints, chicken wire, newspaper, cold-water paste, thick card.

Create a map of an imaginary treasure island. Get the children to make up names for some of the different places – Misty Mountains, Deadman's Swamp, and so on. Ask them to add small drawings showing what they look like. Extend the work by making a class model from paper maché. You will need a sheet of thick card for the base, and some chicken wire or screwed-up newspaper for the relief features. All the children can join in, glueing strips of newspaper to the model and building up different areas. The work will take several weeks to complete as the paper maché should be allowed to dry out at intervals. The final stage is to paint the land and sea and label key features.

Copymasters

1.11 Plan Views This copymaster helps children to relate oblique views and plans. They should colour the pictures and write the correct number in the empty circle next to each plan.

1.12 Route Maze The children should draw a short and long route from home to school, using lines of different colours, and discuss the things they would see on the way.

1.13 Farm Scene This copymaster can be used in two ways. The children should either draw lines linking the small pictures with the correct point in the farm scene, or cut out the small pictures and glue them where they think they belong.

1.14 Adventure Playground The children should colour the six pictures of play equipment, cut them out and arrange them to make their own adventure playground plan.

 Area of Study 5 | **FOLLOW A ROUTE** | CM 1.15 –1.18

 Level 2 | **Statement of Attainment**
2c) Pupils should be able to follow a route using a plan.

Example and links with the Programme of Study
Children should use plans and maps produced by the teacher, other adults or pupils. They should be able to

follow a route around the classroom, school building, school grounds or nearby open space.

Introduction

Time-lapse photographs sometimes show city streets at night so that the headlights of vehicles appear as trails through the darkened streets. These create a visual record of the different routes that cars take as they travel through the city. The routes appear to be haphazard when shown in this way. Similarly, people appear to move haphazardly at a busy railway station, but each takes a route with some personal purpose.

This Statement of Attainment introduces the concept of routes. It concentrates on journeys which the children may make for themselves in the immediate environment, using a map or plan. As they get older, children will study how journeys are directed by landscape features, road systems and public transport. With young children the main aim should be to establish the basic principles of how to follow a route.

There are plenty of opportunities for studying routes in the classroom and school building. This is a good place to begin, as it is an environment which is familiar to the children. When they become more confident and assured you can introduce them to routes in the immediate locality and places further afield.

Key vocabulary

barrier	junction	route
bridge	map	sign
bypass	obstacle	subway
crossing	path	track
door	pattern	trail
gate	plan	way
journey	road	

Key questions

How do people know which route to take?
Is the shortest route always best?
How do barriers and obstacles affect routes?
What happens when routes cross?

Legends

Tell the children the story of Theseus and the Minotaur. Can they make a map showing the route through the maze? How would it have helped Theseus?

Footprints. Get the children to devise a route for others to follow.

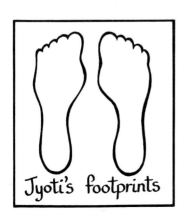

Jyoti's footprints

Picture books

The Snowy Day by Ezra Keats (Bodley Head, 1962) is an award-winning book that describes the effects of heavy snowfall. It illustrates how tracks show up in the snow, and could serve to introduce the idea of routes.

Activity 1.41: Footprints

Materials needed
Paper, light card, scissors, duplicated plans of the classroom.

Get the children to draw the outline of their feet on to a piece of card. They should then cut out the shapes in paper to create footprints, and place these around the class to show different routes. When each child has devised a route, ask them to mark it on a plan of the classroom. See if other children can follow it. What things do they pass on their journey? Do they have to take any sharp turns? If so, why? **Copymaster 1.15** (Tracks) extends the idea by looking at animal tracks.

Activity 1.42: School journeys

Materials needed
Large plan of the school, felt pens.

Make a large plan of the school for a wall display. Use this to record any journeys that the children make around the school during the day. For example, you might ask a child to deliver a message to another class or take the register to the secretary. With your help the children should draw their route on the wall map. Mark each route in a different colour and identify what it represents in a key. Which parts of the school are busiest? Are there any places which the children never seem to visit? Use **Copymaster 1.16** (Routes) to develop the idea that colour helps to pick out or distinguish different routes.

Activity 1.43: Follow the route

Materials needed
Route cards, duplicated plans of the school, class book.

Make a series of route cards for the children to follow. These might ask them to go to the hall, staffroom,

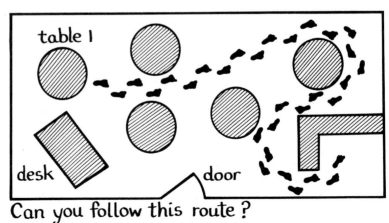

Can you follow this route?

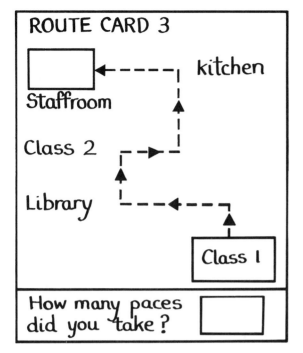

ROUTE CARD 3

Staffroom ← ─ ─ ─ kitchen

Class 2

Library

Class 1

How many paces did you take?

places you have marked using a number system. You might also take photographs for use in a large picture plan when you return to school.

Activity 1.45: Direction signs

Materials needed
Card, felt tips.

Make a study of a direction sign in your locality. Visit it with the children and discuss what it shows. Get them to make careful sketches so that they can make a card model of it when they return to school. Look at maps of your area to find the places named on the sign. Have any of the children been there? Was it a long journey? What other direction signs do they know of?

Activity 1.46: Journeys

Materials needed
Map of the local area, counters.

Help the children to find where they live on a map of the area. You could then ask them to plan a journey to a place of interest. Get them to show the route by placing counters on the map. Could they reach their destination in more than one way? Do they think that the shortest route is bound to be the quickest? Ask them to record their route using **Copymaster 1.17** (Journeys). Plan a number of other journeys to different locations in a similar way.

library, secretary's office and other suitable locations. Get the children to note the things they pass on the way, and the number of paces that they take to reach their destination. When they return to the class, ask the children to mark their route on a duplicated plan of the school. Can they think of any other way of getting to the same place? Was there a short cut that they might have taken? What obstacles got in the way? Mount the plans in a class book to make a route atlas.

Activity 1.44: Street trail

Materials needed
Duplicated sketch maps of the trail route (camera and film – optional).

Devise a simple walk in the area immediately surrounding the school. Write down the main buildings and other places that the children will pass on the route. Mark them on a simple sketch map of the trail and duplicate copies so that every child has one of their own. As the children go round the route, get them to keep track of their position. Ask them whether to turn left or right at junctions. See if they can identify the

Activity 1.47: On the road

Materials needed
Paper, crayons or felt tips.

Ask the children to make a map showing a road linking two places. Get them to add as many details as they like. For example, they could show mountains, rivers, gorges, estuaries, swamps and other natural hazards. You should then ask them to list or describe what you would see on a journey between the two places. Alternatively, you could use **Copymaster 1.18** (On the Road). This takes a similar theme but provides a structure for the children to follow.

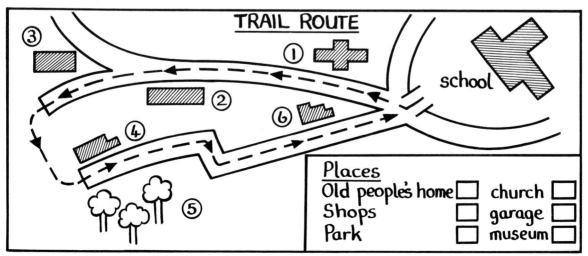

TRAIL ROUTE

school

Places
Old people's home ☐   church ☐
Shops ☐   garage ☐
Park ☐   museum ☐

Copymasters

1.15 Tracks · This copymaster introduces the idea that birds and animals make tracks in the environment. Children should colour the pictures and complete the sentences.

1.16 Routes The children should colour the different routes and write the destinations in the table.

1.17 Journeys This copymaster helps the children to record the route to different points of interest in their area. They should fill in the names of the streets on the routes. There is space for four separate journeys.

1.18 On the Road The children should colour the plan, then circle the things they would see in the table.

RECORD THE WEATHER

CM 1.19 –1.22

Statement of Attainment

Level **2**

2d) Pupils should be able to record weather observations made over a short period.

Example and links with the Programme of Study
The children should observe, describe and record the weather over a period of a day, week or month. They should construct charts and use their own symbols to show wet, dry, hot, windy and calm conditions.

Introduction
The weather has a profound effect on our lives. It influences our moods, the clothes we wear, the houses we live in, and how we spend our spare time. Long-term weather patterns (climates) are even more crucial as they determine the crops that can be grown. It is salutary to remember that we still depend on farming and agriculture for our survival. This is one of the reasons why global warming presents such a serious threat.

In these days of central heating and door-to-door transport, children are often isolated from natural processes. One of the best ways of making them aware of the weather is through direct experience. This is recognised in this Statement of Attainment, which requires children to make their own records and observations. It follows that they will have to undertake some simple fieldwork.

Weather studies can be linked to many other areas of the curriculum, especially science. The variety of the weather, and the effects of weathering on buildings and the landscape could form topics for investigation. The opportunities for introducing art and mathematics will also be apparent.

Key vocabulary

breeze	frost	storm
calm	gale	symbol
chart	hail	thunder
cloud	hot	warm
cold	ice	weather
drizzle	mild	wet
dry	rain	windy
dull	shower	
fog	snow	

Key questions
How does the weather affect us?
How can we record the weather?
Why does the weather change?
Is there a pattern to the weather?
What is the weather like in other places?

Picture books
The Weather Cat by Helen Cresswell (Collins, 1989) is a gentle story about a cat that can forecast the weather. *Cloudy with a Chance of Meat Balls* by Judi Barrett (Gollancz, 1980) is a rather more dramatic tale about a land where it rains food. All goes well until the weather takes a turn for the worse.

Poems and rhymes
There is a range of weather poems in *The Possum Tree* by Lesley Pyott (Black, 1985), as well as in many other anthologies. 'Incey Wincey Spider' is a popular rhyme.

Incey Wincey Spider

Incey wincey spider,
Climbing up the spout;
Down came the rain,
And washed the spider out;

Out came the sun,
And dried up all the rain;
Incey wincey spider,
Climbing up again.

Songs
There is a wide choice of weather songs. One that often proves popular is 'The North Wind Doth Blow' from *The Music Box Songbook* compiled by Barry Gibson (BBC, 1987).

Activity 1.48: Weather words

Materials needed

Photographs from magazines and newspapers, light card.

Make a collection of photographs and pictures from newspapers and magazines showing different types of weather. Talk with the children about what the pictures show. What words would they use to describe the weather conditions? Get the children to write labels to pin under each picture. When they have completed the work, play a game by taking the labels away and asking the children to put them back where they belong.

Activity 1.49: Weather symbols

Materials needed

Small pieces of card, crayons, felt tips and flash cards.

Make a set of flash cards based on weather words such as rain, wind, cloud, sun, snow. Give the children some small pieces of card and ask them to draw symbols to go with each word. Alternatively, you could give them **Copymaster 1.19** (Weather Symbols) to colour and cut out. Use the symbols and flash cards in some simple matching games. Snap and Pelmanism both provide useful models.

Activity 1.50: Experiencing the weather

Materials needed

Sugar paper, scissors, felt tips.

Take the children into the playground and talk with them about the weather. How does it make them feel? Could they describe it to someone far away? When you return to the classroom, get the children to make a large cut-out figure of a person for a wall display. You could ask a child to lie on the floor and get the others to draw round the outline on to sugar paper. Add labels describing the weather. Repeat the same exercise on a

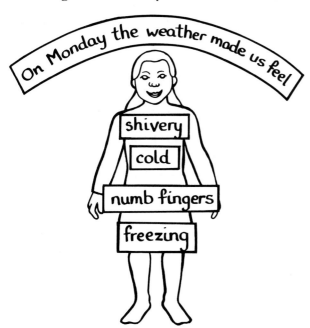

contrasting day later in the week and put up a second display using an outline figure and labels in the same way.

Activity 1.51: All in a day

Make two separate visits to the playground to record the weather, once in the morning and once in the afternoon. Does it feel warm or cold? Is it calm or windy? Ask the children to complete **Copymaster 1.20** (All in a Day). Was there any difference between the morning and afternoon? Discuss what might happen to the weather during the evening.

Activity 1.52: Recording the weather

Materials needed

A large sheet of card, paper, crayons, felt tips, scissors.

Get the children to make a set of words and symbols for different weather conditions. They should draw these on small squares of paper so that they can pin them up on a weather chart. Ask the children to select the correct word and symbol for each different day. At the end of the week add up the totals. Has it been mostly cloudy, sunny, or rainy? You could continue to keep records for a period of a month and enter them into a computer database as part of a project in technology.

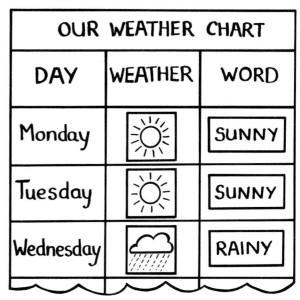

Activity 1.53: Weather dial

Materials needed

Light card, paper fasteners, felt tips and crayons, scissors.

Get the children to make weather dials from light card. The first step is to cut out a house shape with a window on the right-hand side. The children should then cut out a card circle and draw weather symbols around the edge. To assemble the dial they fix the circle behind the house with a paper fastener. As they turn the dial the different symbols will appear. They should set the weather window each day to record different conditions.

45

Weather dial

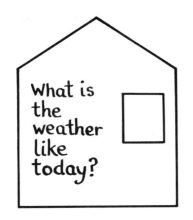

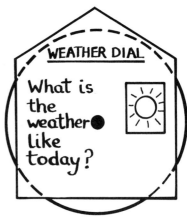

Card house shape with cut-out window   Card circle with weather symbols   Completed dial with paper fastener

Before you begin this activity you might find it helpful to make a dial of your own so that you can show the children what it looks like.

children to make drawings of some of the activities for a class display.

Activity 1.54: Weather forecast

Materials needed
Doll/teddy bear with clothes, question and answer cards.

Bring a doll or teddy bear to school to act as a weather 'forecaster'. Decide on the weather each morning and dress the bear in the correct set of clothes for the day. You could make a set of question and answer cards to include in the display. For example, the question might be 'What's the weather like today, teddy?'. The children then have to select the right answer, such as 'It's warm and sunny'. You might also talk about different ways of forecasting the weather and find out about traditional weather proverbs as part of the work.

Activity 1.55: The right weather

Talk with the children about how the weather affects our lives. Has the weather ever spoilt what they were doing? Can they think of different activities which can only be done if the weather is right? Swimming out of doors and tobogganing are cases in point. Get them to complete **Copymaster 1.21** (The Right Weather) as a way of developing this theme. You might also ask the

Activity 1.56: Wind testers

Materials needed
Balloon, string, paper, scissors, gardening sticks, nails, card, Sellotape.

Make a number of different wind testers to use in the playground. These could include a balloon on a piece of string, a paper fish, a simple windmill and a streamer. Using the testers, find out if there is a strong breeze, light breeze, dead calm, and so on. Which of the devices seems most sensitive? Are some parts of the playground windier than others?

Activity 1.57: Weather picture

Materials needed
General artwork materials including paints and brushes.

Divide a display board into four sections: wet, windy, sunny and cold. Ask the children to paint a picture or make a collage of the type of weather they like most. Pin their work up on the correct part of the display board, together with explanatory sentences such as 'I like windy weather because it's exciting' or 'When it rains I enjoy playing in puddles'.

Wind testers

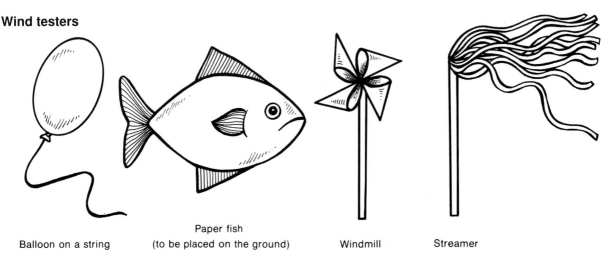

Balloon on a string

Paper fish
(to be placed on the ground)

Windmill

Streamer

46

Activity 1.58: Weather music

Materials needed
Musical instruments.

Compose some different pieces of music with the children to evoke different types of weather. For example, they might choose a lazy summer's day or a storm at sea as their theme. Can they capture this musically? What instruments and sounds are most appropriate? When the composition is complete, invite another class to come and listen to a performance. Can they guess the weather that the children had in mind?

Activity 1.59: World weather

Materials needed
Slides of weather world-wide, pictures from magazines and travel brochures, world map.

Show the children some slides of weather in different parts of the world. Discuss the pictures. What can they tell about each place? Does it look cold or hot? Is it wet or dry? Would the children like to live there? Give them **Copymaster 1.22** (World Weather) to complete. In which part of the world would they expect to find these different weather conditions? Cut up some of the copy-masters and pin the pictures to the correct part of the world map as part of a display on world weather. Add pictures from magazines and travel brochures.

Copymasters

1.19 Weather Symbols The children should colour the symbols on this copymaster and use them in simple matching games such as Snap and Pelmanism. It is best to reproduce the sheet on light card for durability.

1.20 All in a Day This is a recording sheet to help children note changes in the weather during the day. They should write the date at the top, complete the clocks, circle the correct word in each pair and colour the symbol at the bottom that seems most appropriate.

1.21 The Right Weather Get the children to colour the three weather symbols and circle the activities which go with each one. This reinforces the idea that the weather affects our lives.

1.22 World Weather The four pictures illustrate scenes from different parts of the world. The children should colour them and discuss the differences.

 Area of Study 7 **INTERPRET PHOTOGRAPHS** CM 1.23 –1.25

 Level 2 ▷ **Statement of Attainment**
2e) Pupils should be able to identify familiar features on photographs and pictures.

Example and links with the Programme of Study
Children should identify features such as homes, streets, railways, motorways, rivers, hills, woods and fields on pictures and photographs. They should use this information to help them find out about local and distant places.

Introduction
Pictures, slides and photographs are a valuable source of information about places. They supplement field-work observations and can provide a permanent record of the human and physical landscape. This Statement of Attainment directs attention to the use of visual clues and evidence. Through careful questioning it is often possible to use pictures and photographs as a key teaching resource.

Children need help in asking geographical questions. Rather than scanning pictures haphazardly, they should be encouraged to look for categories of information. Useful headings include clothing, trans-port, housing, vegetation and landscape.

To begin with, children can be shown images of their own environment. This will enable them to match the visual evidence with their knowledge and experience. As they become more skilled in the study techniques they can be shown views of more distant locations. It will then be possible to compare similarities and differences. The opportunities for developing and extending geographical vocabulary should also be exploited.

Key vocabulary

bridge	home	river
city	lake	street
factory	marsh	town
farm	motorway	valley
field	mountain	village
forest	place	wood
hill	railway	

Key questions
What are the main landscape features?
Are there any roads and buildings?
What do you think the weather is like?
Would you like to live in this place?

Picture books

Gerry's Seaside Journey by Michelle Cartlidge (Heinemann, 1988) is an enchanting story of a family of teddy bears that moves to the seaside. The pictures and text describe a number of different places, such as city streets, the motorway, a garage and country lanes.

Songs

'A Windmill in Old Amsterdam', from *Apusskidu* by Beatrice Harrop (Black, 1975) is popular.

Activity 1.60: Familiar scenes

Materials needed

Camera and film.

Take some photographs of different features of the local area. Try to include some physical features, such as hills, as well as streets and buildings. Make a display of the photographs and see if the children can recognise them. Ask them to write a sentence saying what each one shows. Encourage them to find out more about each photograph by asking geographical questions. **Copymaster 1.24** (Photograph Survey) will help to structure the work.

Activity 1.61: Fieldwork sketches

Materials needed

Clipboards, pencils, paper, class scrapbook.

Arrange visits to a number of local streets and buildings. Ask the children to make simple field sketches of things that interest them. These could be small details such as door knockers and letter boxes, as well as more general scenes. When you return to school get the children to write a description to go with each drawing and put their work in a class scrapbook. What are the features that identify different streets?

Activity 1.62: Postcards

Materials needed

Postcards, old shoe boxes.

Make a collection of postcards of different places in the United Kingdom and abroad. You could start the collection off with some postcards of your own, but the children should also be invited to contribute. Put out some old shoe boxes so that the children can sort the cards into groups. Label the boxes with different headings such as 'towns', 'beaches' and 'mountains'. By changing the headings you can vary the exercise. For example, you might get the children to sort the cards into summer and winter scenes.

Activity 1.63: Other countries

Materials needed

Pictures from magazines.

Make a display of pictures from magazines showing different places around the world. These could include cities, motorways, forests, deserts and villages. Discuss the pictures with the children. What do they show? Is it a place in our own country, or is it somewhere overseas? Use **Copymaster 1.25** (Different Places) to get the children to analyse the pictures in greater detail.

Activity 1.64: Comparisons

Materials needed

Two contrasting pictures or photographs.

Select two contrasting pictures or photographs of different places. Working as a class, get the children to list the different features they can see. Pin the pictures and words on a display board with a space in between. Now write down all the features of your own area in the centre of the display. Finally, make a comparison between the lists. How many features of your own area correspond with features in the places in the pictures? Draw lines linking them together.

THE SWISS ALPS

Features
1 _____
2 _____
3 _____
4 _____

OUR OWN AREA

Features
1 _____
2 _____
3 _____
4 _____
5 _____

DEVON COAST

Features
1 _____
2 _____
3 _____
4 _____

Compare pictures of different places.

Activity 1.65: Picture viewer

Materials needed
Tracing paper, library books.

Make a display of books from the school library that have pictures of mountains, rivers, towns, villages and other geographical features. Talk with the children about what they can see. Encourage close observation by getting them to make a simple picture viewer by drawing a grid on tracing paper, or some other transparent material. The grid should divide the picture into four sections – near and distant, left and right. What can the children find in each section? Can they imagine what the things in the distance might look like from close to?

Activity 1.66: Copying pictures

Materials needed
Pictures of different places, tracing paper, card, sticky-back plastic.

Mount some pictures of different places on card and cover them with sticky-back plastic for protection. Ask the children to choose a picture that interests them and to copy the main features using a piece of tracing paper. You should stress that they only need to show the outline shapes. To complete the exercise get them to colour their pictures and list the things they have shown.

Activity 1.67: Library quiz

Materials needed
Library books, quiz cards.

Select some library books which have a variety of pictures showing places around the world. Devise some quiz cards to go with the books. For example, you might ask the children which book has a picture of the River Nile in it, or what they can see on the cover of a given book. You could turn this activity into a game in which the children describe a picture as clearly as they can without naming it, while the others guess what it is. Both approaches will help to extend the children's geographical vocabulary and enhance their powers of visual discrimination.

Copymasters

1.23 Town and Country The children should colour the two different scenes. This will introduce the idea that pictures provide information about places.

1.24 Photograph Survey This copymaster will help children to analyse features in photographs. It is best if they begin by looking at scenes from the local area before progressing to more distant locations.

1.25 Different Places Children should use the checklist of physical and human features in this copymaster to help them study pictures of different places.

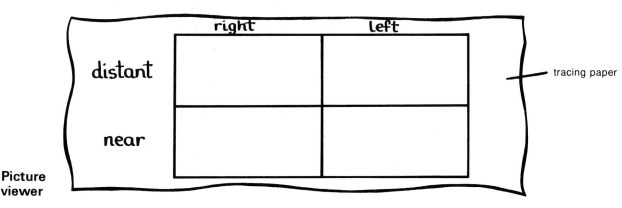

Picture viewer

WORKING TOWARDS LEVEL 3

Programme of Study	School-based work	Contrasting area	World dimension
Pupils should be taught to use the eight points of the compass.	What landmarks lie in different directions from your school? What is the direction of the wind today?	Do the roads and railways spread out equally in all directions from here? Which direction do the rivers flow in?	Which countries lie in different compass directions from the United Kingdom? How are compass directions used in names and everyday speech? (e.g. sou'wester)
Pupils should be taught to make a map of a short route, showing main features in the correct order.	How do you know your way round the school? Can you make a school journey map that other children can follow?	What are the main landmarks? How are they shown on a map? Can you put them in order to make a puzzle?	What places would you pass on a specific journey a) by boat? b) by air? Can you devise some journeys from the United Kingdom to other destinations?
Pupils should be taught to use letter and number co-ordinates to locate features on maps.	Can you add letter and number co-ordinates to a classroom or school map? What things are found in specified squares?	How are co-ordinates used on area and Ordnance Survey maps? What are the co-ordinates of specific features?	How are co-ordinates used on atlas maps? What are the equator, prime meridian and tropics? What are the northern and southern hemispheres?
Pupils should be taught to locate their own position and identify features using a large-scale map.	Can you find your place on a plan of the classroom? Can you name the different rooms and features on a school plan?	What landscape features are shown on a map of the locality? What places and buildings are named?	What is the shape of the United Kingdom? Where is the United Kingdom on the world map? What are the main features of the world map?
Pupils should be taught to identify features on oblique aerial photographs.	What is the shape of your school from the air? What details of your school show up in an aerial photograph?	Are there any rivers, lakes or seas? Are there any woods, marshes or moors? Are there any car parks, railway lines or tunnels?	What does the earth look like from space? What do satellite pictures show us?

ATTAINMENT TARGET 2: KNOWLEDGE AND UNDERSTANDING OF PLACES

Pupils should demonstrate their increasing knowledge and understanding of places in local, regional, national, international and global contexts, particularly:

i) a knowledge of places;
ii) an understanding of the distinctive features that give a place its identity;
iii) an understanding of the similarities and differences between places; and
iv) an understanding of the relationship between themes and issues in particular locations.

Programme of Study for Key Stage 1 (Levels 1 & 2 only. For Level 3 see p. 76)

Places and themes

5 Pupils should develop their awareness of localities in and beyond their own country. *Where possible such teaching should build on pupils' experience from visits, but should also use secondary sources, for example, photographs, objects, stories, videos and accounts by teachers and other adults.*

A locality should be a small area with distinctive features and in the case of the local area is the immediate vicinity of the school or of where the pupil lives.

6 Pupils should be taught:
   - to name where they live;
   - to name the country in which they live;
   - that their own country is part of the United Kingdom, which is made up of England, Wales, Scotland and Northern Ireland.

8 During Key Stage 1 pupils should study:
   - the local area;
   - a locality in the United Kingdom which offers a contrast to the local area;
   - a locality beyond the United Kingdom.

These localities should also be used as appropriate for work towards Attainment Targets 3, 4 and 5.

9 Pupils should be taught to:
   - identify and name familiar features in the local area, *for example, buildings, parks, places of worship;*
   - investigate the use of land and buildings in the local area;
   - talk about work and leisure activities, *for example, investigate where people go to enjoy themselves and to work;*
   - investigate features of localities outside the local area, *for example, through looking at holiday postcards and photographs;* identify the features of, and talk about, places outside the local area; and investigate how these features might affect people's lives;
   - identify and describe similarities and differences between their local area and other localities.

ABOUT THIS ATTAINMENT TARGET ▶

One way of teaching children about places is to build on and extend their knowledge of the immediate environment. This is bound to be the area that they know best. The immediate environment also illustrates ideas on a scale relative to the children's understanding, and shows how different forces interact. These different elements are all reflected in this Attainment Target.

In making a study of places, children need a grounding in locational knowledge. In other words, they need to be able to identify plans and physical features on a map. The working party that devised the National Curriculum kept this requirement to a minimum. The places and landscape features that they specified are designed to provide a simple framework to which other information can be added. At Level 1 and 2 the demands are extremely light. Children only have to know their own address and be able to name the countries of the United Kingdom.

However, geography involves much more than just naming places. It involves understanding connections and relationships. The National Curriculum specifies the different areas which children have to study. At Key Stage 1 infants are required to investigate (a) the local area; (b) a contrasting locality in the United Kingdom; (c) a locality beyond the United Kingdom. Within these constraints teachers are free to select any place of their choice. They are also invited to incorporate themes from the other Attainment Targets into their schemes of work.

The study of distant locations is one of the most challenging demands in the geography National Curriculum. It will take time to develop the necessary resources and expertise. Postcards, photographs, slides, objects, videos, first-hand accounts and stories are all valuable sources of information. There may also be opportunities to set up links with other schools, either elsewhere in the United Kingdom or abroad, so that children can provide resources for each other.

BACKGROUND INFORMATION FOR THE TEACHER ▶

Geography is a practical subject. It relates to specific places and locations. These range from rainforests and forests to grasslands and icecaps. All over the world people have found ways of exploiting their environment. Case studies at a variety of different levels, from the local to the international, are one of the best ways of illustrating this.

A knowledge of places
We all naturally tend to place ourselves at the centre of the world. We have a detailed knowledge of our immediate surroundings, but our image of more distant places is less distinct. It is impossible to specify all the places which children might need to know about. However, if they have a framework of locational knowledge this will provide them with a valuable structure.

Features which give a place its identity
Most people feel an affinity for the places they know well. Even if the environment is unremarkable, memories and associations help to give it meaning. On a national level, people develop a love of their homeland. This then becomes enshrined in the poetry, literature and songs which help to make up a culture. Personal feelings and reactions are involved, as well as objective facts about settlements and landscapes.

Similarities and differences between places
Differences in climate, vegetation and geology around the world influence the way people live their lives. At the same time, the basic needs of clothing, food and shelter serve to unify the human race. Individual circumstances may lead to different solutions but the objectives tend to be the same. Children should think about both the similarities and the differences when they do their studies.

Relationship between themes and issues
The relationship between themes and issues is a complex matter. It is best illustrated in case studies, and is often particularly evident in environmental problems. The nuclear accident at Chernobyl, for example, involved a mixture of human and physical factors. The siting of the plant, and the wind and atmospheric conditions at the time provided a setting in which the decision to build a nuclear power station and human error in operating it were played out. Deforestation, desertification and global warming all involve a similar mixture of forces.

Facts and figures about the United Kingdom
● The mainland of the United Kingdom is the eighth largest island in the world.

● The Severn is the longest river in the United Kingdom (354 km).

● Ben Nevis is the highest mountain (1343 m).

● Lough Neagh in Northern Ireland is the largest lake.

● The population of the United Kingdom was 57 million in 1989.

● London is the largest city, with over 7.5 million people.

NAME LOCAL FEATURES

CM 2.1
–2.3

Statement of Attainment

Level **1**

1a) Pupils should be able to name familiar features of the local area.

Example and links with the Programme of Study

Children should be able to name local rivers, hills, woods and parks. They should also be aware of features of the built environment, such as roads, post boxes, shops and places of worship.

Introduction

Geographers are concerned with the study of places. They consider physical features, they look at the way people have used the environment, and they analyse the issues and conflicts that arise. This Statement of Attainment lays the foundations for these investigations by introducing young children to key features in their immediate surroundings.

There are many ways of helping children to learn to name familiar places. As well as identifying them from different types of evidence, they can be asked to sort them into various categories. This will develop their vocabulary and heighten their awareness of the local area.

The ability to communicate is as essential in geography as it is in any other academic subject. Accurate naming and labelling is a basic skill. It is best developed in a familiar context, and the local area makes an ideal starting point.

Key vocabulary

bridge	park
bus stop	playground
church	post box
crossing	pub
field	railway
garden	road
hill	school
hotel	shop
house	street
local	telephone box
office	wood

Key questions

What are the main buildings in the local area?
Are there any rivers, hills, woods or other physical features?
What are the names of local landmarks?
Can they be put into categories or groups?

Picture books

Wilberforce Goes to Playgroup by Margaret Gordon (Penguin, 1987) is one of a series of stories about Wilberforce the bear, all of which are set in an everyday environment. The pictures are full of details for the children to observe and discuss.

Poems and rhymes

Our Village by John Yeoman (Walker, 1988) is an illustrated book of modern poems about traditional rural life. The following rhyme is also appropriate:

Round and Round the Garden

Round and round the garden,
Like a teddy bear;
One step, two steps,
Tickle him under there.

Songs

'What's it like in the place where you live?' from *Songs from Play School* (Black, 1987) is ideal for this Statement of Attainment.

Activity 2.1: Familiar features

Materials needed
Photographs of features in the vicinity of the school.

Talk with the children about familiar features in the vicinity of the school. What are the things they notice? What makes them special? Ask the children to make drawings of some of them. It is helpful to have a collection of photographs of local features to refer to. You could prepare this collection beforehand, or you could take the pictures during an environmental walk with the class. Use **Copymaster 2.1** (In the Street) to extend the work. This is designed to reinforce basic vocabulary.

Activity 2.2: Places snap

Materials needed
Photographs of familiar features in the locality, labels and light card.

Take a set of photographs of familiar features in the immediate locality and mount them on light card. Now make a set of card labels of the same size, naming each feature. Use the photographs and labels to play places snap. You will need to show the children all the photographs and labels before they begin the game. They will consolidate their knowledge of local places as they play it.

Activity 2.3: Picture map

Materials needed
Large-scale map of the local area.

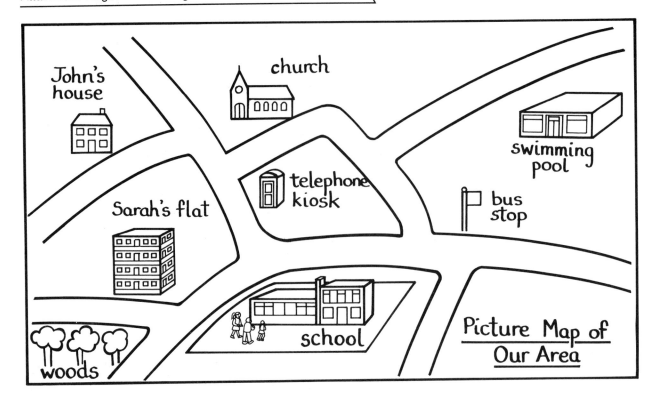

Draw a large-scale map of the local area as a wall display. Begin with just an outline of the local streets. Get the children to identify the position of the school and see how many different places they can name. Ask them to make drawings of familiar features to add to the map. They might show their own homes, local churches, traffic lights, shops, street signs, and so on. Discuss the map with the whole class. What impression does it give of your neighbourhood? Are there things which have been missed out?

Activity 2.4: Landmarks

Materials needed

Frieze paper, scissors, crayons, glue.

Consider the landmarks which different people notice. Car drivers see road signs, elderly people know where to find seats and benches, tourists look out for museums and other attractions. Develop this idea using **Copymaster 2.2** (Landmarks). The children should colour the pictures, cut them out and arrange them as a frieze. They might also add some drawings of their own.

Activity 2.5: Places alphabet

Materials needed

Pieces of light card.

Working as a class, make a list of all the places you can think of in the local area. Get the children to write a label for each one on a piece of card. Mount these in alphabetical order as a class display. Extend the work by asking the children to complete **Copymaster 2.3** (Places Alphabet). There are spaces for eight letters on the sheet. You could either choose these beforehand or let the children make their own selection.

Activity 2.6: Guide book

Materials needed

Photographs of local features, glue, class book.

Make a guide book for your local area. You will need to collect a range of different photographs or pictures of local features for the children to use. Get them to name each one and mount it in a class book, together with a caption. If there is any spare space you could include some drawings which the children have made. These are best made on site as part of an organised visit or outing.

Activity 2.7: Landmark models

Materials needed

Photographs of local landmarks, Plasticine.

Give the children photographs of some local landmarks and ask them to model them in Plasticine. You could arrange the models on a display board with captions or labels. Alternatively, you could display them alongside the photographs. See if the children can think of any other landmarks that they would like to add.

Activity 2.8: Places quiz

Materials needed
Quiz cards, empty shoe box.

Make a series of quiz cards which involve local landmarks and other features. For example, you might ask the children to name the local park, or the nearest street with a post box. You could put the questions in a special quiz box for the children to use in conjunction with the class guide book (see Activity 2.6).

Copymasters

2.1 In the Street The children should colour the pictures and complete the captions using the words from the top of the page.

2.2 Landmarks Each of the people shown on the copymaster is associated with a particular landmark. The children should colour the pictures, cut them out and place the people and buildings together in a frieze.

2.3 Places Alphabet The children should write different letters in the empty circles and name places in the local area which begin with those letters. Alternatively, you could write the letters on the sheet beforehand.

 Area of Study 2

ACTIVITIES IN THE LOCAL AREA

 CM 2.4 –2.7

Level 1	**Statement of Attainment**
	1b) Pupils should be able to identify activities carried out by people in the local area.

Example and links with the Programme of Study
Children should talk about where people go for work and leisure. They should find out about the jobs done in school and investigate how services are provided in the community.

Introduction
This Statement of Attainment requires children to observe people at work, and introduces them to the idea of human interdependence.

Most infants have very little idea of what people do when they go to work. The impression that they gain by watching adults at school (most of whom exercise a form of parental care) is rather misleading.

Young children will need assistance in drawing conclusions from what they observe. For example, the postman does not merely walk from house to house; he delivers letters. It is important to move beyond what is immediately obvious. The challenge in teaching this Statement of Attainment is to ensure that children develop the appropriate concepts and vocabulary.

Key vocabulary

caretaker	factory	school
church	helper	secretary
cinema	librarian	sports centre
cleaner	nurse	teacher
cook	painter	theatre
dentist	park	vicar
doctor	policeman	visitor

Key questions
Why do people do jobs?
Do people always get paid for work?
How do jobs differ?
Do jobs always stay the same?

Picture books
Mrs Jolly's Joke Shop by Allan Ahlberg and Colin McNaughton (Penguin, 1988) provides a light-hearted introduction to both work and leisure.

Poems and rhymes
If you want to consider the adults that work in a school, *Please Mrs Butler* by Allan Ahlberg (Kestrel, 1983) is a good resource. *Mother Goose Comes to Cable Street* by Rosemary Stones and Andrew Mann (Kestrel, 1977) takes a different approach. It is a collection of modern nursery rhymes, and is beautifully illustrated with evocative drawings of many different parts of London.

Activity 2.9: School jobs
Talk with the children about the different people who work in your school. Discuss what jobs they do. Make lists of (a) people who work in school every day and (b) people who visit the school. **Copymaster 2.4** (School Jobs) is designed to prompt ideas. You should check that the children can read the words and understand what they mean before they begin.

CARETAKER

Name : Mr James

Job : Looks after the school building

Begins work : 7·00

Finishes work : 6·00

Place of work : All round the school

Activity 2.10: Job fact files

Materials needed
Rectangles of light card in different colours.

Make a display of fact files about the different jobs done in your school. Each fact file should give the name of the person, the job that they do, the hours that they work and the part of the building that they use. The children should collect this information by conducting simple interviews. They could also make drawings of each person to go with the fact files in the display. **Copymaster 2.5** (Counting the Jobs) provides a supporting activity.

Activity 2.11: Tools and equipment

Materials needed
Paintbrush, spanner, piece of chalk, calculator, cleaning cloth.

Set up a small display of equipment that different people use as part of their job. Let the children examine the different items and talk about what they think they are. Who might use them and why? How do tools and equipment help us in our work? Which jobs require lots of equipment? Which ones require hardly any? Ask the children to complete **Copymaster 2.6** (Equipment) to extend and consolidate the work.

Activity 2.12: Running a school

Materials needed
Sugar paper, felt tips.

Make a list of the things which are needed to keep a school going. This might include electricity, gas, water, telephones, books, food, repairs and emergency services. Put the list up on the wall as a display. Ask the children to decide who provides these different things. Make a list of jobs in a separate column.

Activity 2.13: Advertisements

Materials needed
Advertisements for different services, class book.

Make a collection of advertisements for different services. You could start this off yourself and get the children to add to the collection using newspapers, brochures and the *Yellow Pages*. Put the advertisements into a class directory. Ask the children to add an advertisement of their own for a service that they can provide. In any class there are a surprising number of children who are 'expert' in one thing or another. Those who are not can always make something up.

Activity 2.14: Street work

Materials needed
Light card, Sellotape, glue.

Ask the children to look carefully at the things they see on their way to and from school. How many people do they see who are doing a job? What work are they doing? Are they always working in the same place, or do they move around? Make a concertina book for the children to display their notes and drawings in. You can add to this over a period of time as the children notice more and more things. You could also make a

DIFFERENT JOBS

pictures of people at work

quiz questions

concertina book

QUIZ

simple quiz to go with it. The questions might ask 'Who uses a ladder?' 'Who uses a hard hat?' 'Who works from a van?', and so on.

Activity 2.15: Mime a job

Ask the children to mime a job which they have seen someone doing. They might do this individually during a movement lesson, or they could perform in front of others, working in groups. Can the children who are watching guess the job? Can they think of any jobs that require teamwork? Ask them to mime these as a small tableau or scene.

Activity 2.16: Time to spare

Materials needed

Rectangles of light card, three buckets.

Talk with the children about the places in the local area where people go to enjoy themselves. Examples might include the cinema, theatre, bowling alley, swimming pool, sports centre, football pitches, recreation ground, church hall, and so on. Make labels for each of these places on rectangular strips of card. Now put three buckets in the middle of the class. The first is for places where only adults can go to enjoy themselves, the second for places used by both

children and adults, and the third for places that are only used by children. Get the children to put the labels in the correct bucket. They can then record their results using **Copymaster 2.7** (Time to Spare).

Copymasters

2.4 School Jobs   The children should complete the lists of jobs which are done in their school. This might be best approached as a class exercise. The children might add the following: teacher, cook, dinner lady, cleaner, classroom helper, road crossing supervisor, parents, librarian, police officer, vicar, dentist, photographer.

2.5 Counting the Jobs   Working as a group or class, the children should colour a square for each person they can think of doing each job. The completed sheets will show a bar graph.

2.6 Equipment   The children should draw lines from each item of equipment to the person they think would use it. They could use two different colours to highlight the difference.

2.7 Time to Spare   Use this copymaster in conjunction with Activity 2.16. The children should write down the different places that people go to in their leisure time in the correct circle or 'bucket'.

<table>
<tr><td>Area of Study 3</td><td>**STATE WHERE THEY LIVE**</td><td>CM 2.8 –2.11</td></tr>
</table>

Level 1	**Statement of Attainment**
	1c) Pupils should be able to state where they live.

Example and links with the Programme of Study

Children should be able to state the number of their house or dwelling, the name of their street, and the name of the town, district or village where they live.

Introduction

We all tend to define the world in relation to our own particular position. For example, most world maps published in Europe show Europe in a prominent place in the centre of the world. In other continents, however, people have a different perspective. Australians, for instance, find it more useful to focus on their own country and to show Europe on the edge of the world map.

Young children are especially egocentric. The place where they live is the centre of their world. This Statement of Attainment recognises this, and requires them to state their own address. Among other things, this is important for safety reasons.

On the face of it, the Statement of Attainment seems extremely simple. However, children need to understand that there are different elements in an address. The house, street and settlement are identified systematically in a given order. This implies a hierarchy. Postcodes are composed in a similar way, but are even more complex as they consist of combinations of letters and numbers.

Key vocabulary

address	house
area	lane
avenue	name
close	number
code	odd
country	road
district	street
envelope	town
even	village
hill	

Key questions

Why do houses have numbers?
What can we learn from street names?
Why are addresses written on more than one line?
Do addresses ever change?

Songs

'I have a Little Tiny House' from *The Music Box Storybook* (BBC, 1987) is recommended.

Activity 2.17: Envelopes

Materials needed
A collection of used envelopes, pictures of post boxes, Post Office vans and postal workers.

Make a collection of envelopes that are delivered to school. Get the children to add some envelopes of their own. What are the differences between the addresses? How does the postman know which house to go to? Put the envelopes up in a display, together with drawings or photographs of post boxes, Post Office vans and postal workers.

Activity 2.18: Your address

Materials needed
Used postage stamps, glue.

Talk with the children about the different parts of an address. Explain that, in the UK, the name always comes first, followed by the house number, street, town, county and postcode.

Get the children to write down their own address using **Copymaster 2.8** (My Address). Complete the exercise by cutting out the 'envelopes' and glueing a used postage stamp in the top right-hand corner.

Activity 2.19: Animal addresses

Make up addresses for a number of different animals. You could prompt the children by talking about the habitats that creatures require. You will also find that animal stories provide a stimulus. For example, Bilbo Baggins' address is given in the opening pages of *The Hobbit*. Once they have got the idea, the children should be encouraged to make up addresses of their own.

Activity 2.20: House numbers

Talk about how people identify specific houses. In some places houses are given names, but numbers are much more common. Ask the children the number of their own house. Are the houses in their street numbered sequentially, or are they divided into odd and even? Working as a class, get the children to call out their house numbers. Record these on **Copymaster 2.9** (Odd and Even).

Activity 2.21: Front doors

Materials needed
Clipboards, paper and pencils.

Arrange a visit to a street near your school where the children can see the front doors of the houses from the

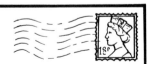

Animal addresses. Get the children to invent addresses for different animals.

pavement. Ask them to make careful drawings, paying special attention to the number, door handle and letter box. Mount the drawings as a display when you return to school. Alternatively, you could give the children **Copymaster 2.10** (My Front Door) to complete at home with the help of their parents.

Activity 2.22: Streets

Materials needed

Large-scale map of the local area map, pins, photographs of street name plates.

Pin a large-scale map of the local area on to the classroom wall. Get the children to find the street where they live and mark it with a pin. Ask them to write the different names in the style of a road name plate, and add these to the display. It is helpful if you have some photographs for the children to copy.

Activity 2.23: Street names

Talk with the children about local street names. Are they named after geographical features (such as hills), famous people, places, or different animals? If they had to make up a name for a new street near the school, what would they choose? Find out more about where the children live using **Copymaster 2.11** (Street Names). Ask individual children to call out the name of their street, while the rest colour in a box in the correct column.

Activity 2.24: Name rubbings

Materials needed

Set of template letters, wax crayons of different colours, plasticine.

Cut out a set of template letters from a sheet of card. Ask the children to use these to make up a name plate for their street. Get them to fix the letters down loosely with plasticine so that they can take a rubbing. You can then mount the rubbings on the wall as a class display. If you give the children crayons of different colours they can experiment with different effects. You can also use a variety of different papers to create extra interest and contrast.

Activity 2.25: Post office

Materials needed

Pens, pencils, forms, envelopes, used stamps, play money.

Set up a post office in a corner of the classroom. It will need a counter, and table tops for the customers to write on. Equip the post office with pens, pencils, forms, envelopes, stamps and play money. Allow the children to play at being customers and counter clerks. They might also make up letters and parcels for posting.

Activity 2.26: Letter post

Materials needed

Large cardboard box, paint, blank envelopes.

Get the children to make a class post box. This could be made from a large cardboard box and painted red using poster paint. Ask each child to address an envelope with their name, table number, class number and school name. When they finish they should post the letters in the box. Collections can be made at a regular time each day and the letters taken to the post office (see Activity 2.25) for sorting. Appoint different children to do the deliveries. You might be able to make (or find) a hat that they can use while they are doing the rounds.

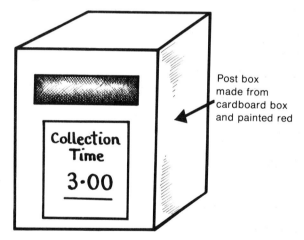

Post box made from cardboard box and painted red

Activity 2.27: Postcodes

Talk to the children about postcodes. What are they, and why do we need them? Do any of the children know their postcode? You could make up a postcode for your class. Devise an abbreviation for your school using two letters, add your class number and finally get the children to add their own table number. This will introduce the idea of systematic numbering and show the children how a postcode can be used as an address.

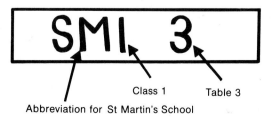

Abbreviation for St Martin's School   Class 1   Table 3

Copymasters

2.8 My Address The children should write their address in the empty boxes and cut out the 'envelope' for a class display. You could use the last box for the postcode rather than the county if you prefer.

2.9 Odd and Even Use this copymaster to record different house numbers as each child calls out where they live in turn. It is essential that they understand the difference between odd and even numbers before they begin.

2.10 My Front Door The children should make a careful drawing of their own front door on this sheet, and answer the questions by writing in the empty spaces.

2.11 Street Names Make a survey of local street names using this copymaster. The children colour one square in the correct column as each child calls out where they live. If the children run out of spaces you should either issue them with a second sheet or stop the survey at that point.

| Area of Study 4 | # THE WIDER WORLD | CM 2.12 –2.14 |

Statement of Attainment

Level **1**

1d) Pupils should be able to demonstrate an awareness of the world beyond their local area.

Example and links with the Programme of Study
The children should talk about places they have visited, and find out about other places by looking at pictures and photographs.

Introduction
Young children often have curious and distorted ideas of the world beyond their local area. Nowadays most children visit places outside the immediate vicinity, but even those who have travelled widely tend to gain only superficial impressions of different places. The motorway network removes features and 'staging posts' from journeys, and air travel to cosmopolitan holiday resorts gives children a false impression of the distance covered.

This Statement of Attainment seeks to develop children's understanding of the wider world. Teachers are encouraged to build on the child's own experience and to use pictures, slides, television programmes and other resources. It takes time for children to develop their concepts of other places. Ultimately they need to understand where they belong in a broader national and international context.

Key vocabulary

clothes	journey
cold	language
country	people
dry	place
food	travel
holiday	weather
hot	wet
house	world

Key questions
In what way is a particular place different?
What is the weather like?
What plants and animals live there?
How do people live their lives there?

Folk tales
Anthologies of folk tales can provide a useful way of introducing this Statement of Attainment. Older children may enjoy *Tikkatoo's Journey* by Amanda Loverseed (Blackie, 1990), which is a beautifully illustrated Eskimo tale.

Picture books
There is a variety of picture books that are set in overseas locations. *A Nice Walk in the Jungle* by Nan Bodsworth (Kestrel, 1989) is particularly noteworthy. *Percy Short and Cuthbert* by Susie Jenkin Pearce (Viking, 1990) is another story not to be missed.

Songs
'The World is Big, The World is Small', from *Tinderbox* (Black, 1982) is recommended.

Activity 2.28: Food

Materials needed
Food labels, packets, tins and jars of food from other countries.

Talk with the children about the different meals they eat. Make a class list of food. Does any of it come from foreign countries? How do we know? Set up a display of food and labels from places overseas, and encourage the children to add items of their own over a period of a week or two.

Activity 2.29: Clothes

Materials needed

Pieces of fabric of different textures and colours, scissors, glue, pictures of people in different costumes.

Discuss the different clothes that we wear. Why do we need a variety of clothes? How do we deal with very cold, hot or wet weather? Look at pictures of people in other parts of the world. What do their clothes tell us about the weather? **Copymasters 2.12** and **2.13** (Clothes 1 and 2) provide outlines which the children can 'dress' using pieces of fabric. When they have completed the sheets they should cut round the outlines and display them on a triangular cardboard stand.

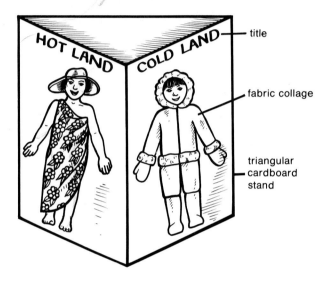

Activity 2.30: House shapes

Materials needed

Strips of coloured card, sugar paper, plastic Meccano/construction kit, pictures of houses worldwide.

Consider different homes around the world. Show the children pictures or slides of a number of different examples. Draw their attention to the shape. Some houses have pitched roofs, others have flat roofs. Some are basically horizontal, others are vertical. Ask the children to make collage pictures using **Copymaster 2.14** (House Shapes), or get them to create models working with plastic Meccano or another construction kit. What shape are the houses in your own area?

Activity 2.31: Holidays

Materials needed

Posters, books and travel brochures, paint, paper.

Set up a display of posters, books and travel brochures showing different holiday destinations. Try to include as wide a range as possible, with cities, beaches, mountains, safari parks, and so on. Let the children select a holiday of their choice. Why did they choose it? What makes it special? Ask them to paint a picture of the place they would like to visit, and put up their work as part of a class display.

Activity 2.32: Travellers

Invite someone who has lived or travelled in a foreign country to talk to the class. You may find that the children's parents or other members of staff will be able to put you in contact with a suitable person. Ideally they should know the place well and be able to describe it in some detail. It also helps if they have experience of talking to infants. Get the children to prepare their questions beforehand. They should try to find out about a wide range of topics such as food, clothes, customs, animals, weather and natural features.

Activity 2.33: Soft toys

Materials needed

A collection of soft toy animals.

Ask the children to bring their soft toys to school. Put these out on display for the class to look at. How many of the creatures would be found in this country? How many come from abroad? Can the children think of any other way of sorting them into groups? Hot and cold places, and land and water provide some other possible

divisions. Get the children to write labels for their toys, saying where they might come from. You could include a world map as part of the display and encourage the children to identify some of the main habitats, such as the icecaps and rainforests.

Activity 2.34: Different scenes

Materials needed
General artwork materials.

Get the children to make a large class collage of a scene from another part of the world. This might be inspired by a visit from someone who has lived abroad, a television programme or a picture book. It does not necessarily need to be outside the United Kingdom. For example, if your school is in a town or city the picture might show a country scene, or vice versa. Whatever you choose should prompt discussion and help to enlarge the children's view of the world.

Activity 2.35: World museum

Materials needed
Pictures and artefacts from different parts of the world.

Set up a display table of pictures and artefacts from different parts of the world. Put labels next to each object. These might say where it came from, for example 'Jennifer brought this from Paris', or might describe how it is used, for example, 'This comb is used in making carpets'. When the children are familiar with the display you could remove the labels and see if the children can replace them again. You might also get them to make drawings of the different objects.

Activity 2.36: World music

Materials needed
Tape recorder, cassettes of music from around the world.

Introduce the children to traditional music from different parts of the world. You will need a tape recorder and a selection of cassettes. Your local record

library may be able to help. Play the children some suitable extracts and talk about the differences in the style of the music. Is the music joyful or sad? When do you think it might be played? What images does it conjure up?

Activity 2.37: Different languages

Materials needed
Labels, tickets, stamps, coins and books in European languages, a map of Europe.

Make a display of labels, tickets, stamps, coins and books written in European languages. Discuss the different European languages with the class. Do any of the children know a foreign language? Can they say a few foreign words which they can translate into English? Talk about where each language is spoken, using a map of Europe.

Copymasters

2.12 and 2.13 Clothes (1 and 2) The children should dress the template figures using scraps of fabric of different texture, and colours. When they have finished they should cut round the outline and mount their work on a triangular stand.

2.14 House Shapes Children can either colour the shapes or stick strips of card on the outlines, which can then be mounted on sugar paper.

 Area of Study 5 | # NAME THEIR OWN COUNTRY | CM 2.15 –2.18

Statement of Attainment

 Level 1

1e) Pupils should be able to name the country in which they live.

Example and links with the Programme of Study
The children should know that their local area is part of a much larger area known as a country, and that this has a specific name.

Introduction
There are over 170 countries in the world. These vary in size from vast countries such as the USA to tiny states such as Singapore. They all have a capital city,

which is usually the centre of government.

This Statement of Attainment requires children to name the country in which they live. It extends Attainment Target 1c), requiring pupils to 'state where they live', and leads directly into Attainment Target 2a), requiring pupils to 'name the countries of the United Kingdom'. In view of these close links it may not be possible to tackle these statements individually.

When children learn the name of their country, it is an appropriate moment to teach them to recognise its shape on a map. This is an important skill which is essential for atlas work. In addition, you might get the children to consider the idea of borders and how they can be represented on a map. These activities will help children to understand why countries are significant units, and how they differ from one another.

Key vocabulary

border	island
capital	map
city	Northern Ireland
coast	Scotland
country	sea
edge	shape
England	Wales

Key questions

What is the shape of your country?
Does it have a coast?
Does it have a land border?
Which countries is it next to?

Activity 2.38: Map exhibition

Materials needed
A variety of different maps of the United Kingdom.

Make an exhibition of different maps of the United Kingdom. You could use brochures, posters, atlases, reference books and other sources. Discuss what the maps show and get the children to describe how they vary. Can the children recognise their own country? What is it called? Extend the work using **Copymaster 2.15** (Which Country?).

Activity 2.39: Name plates

Materials needed
Magazines and colour supplements, card, scissors, glue, sugar paper.

Give the children a set of magazines and colour supplements. Get them to cut out letters to make the name of their country. They could look for interesting and unusual scripts. Ask the children to mount their 'name plates' on sugar paper and put them up on the wall as a display.

Activity 2.40: Name display

Materials needed
A variety of objects displaying the name of your country.

Set up a display table with a variety of objects, all of which feature the name of your country. These may be small items with the words 'Made in . . .' on the bottom, or tourists' souvenirs, such as brochures and tea towels. Can the children find the country name on each thing? Why has it been put there?

Activity 2.41: Acrostic

Materials needed
Squares of card and sugar paper.

Write the letters which spell the name of your country on separate squares of card. Ask the children to arrange them in the correct order, and then attach them to a sheet of sugar paper in a vertical line. Now ask the children to think of an item that comes from your country which begins with each different letter. Write these next to the appropriate letter, together with a simple drawing or picture. If the children want to complete an acrostic of their own you could give them copies of **Copymaster 2.16** (Acrostic). This has been devised for England but could easily be adapted for Wales, Scotland or Ireland by changing the words and letters. You could also ring the changes by making up an acrostic using place names from your own area.

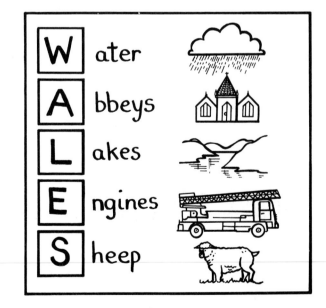

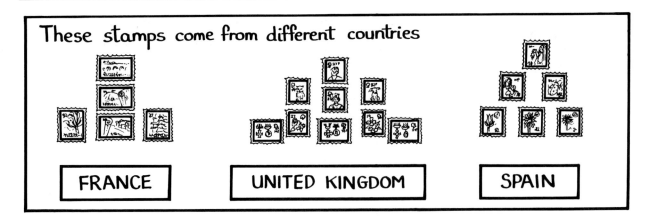

Activity 2.42: Jigsaw puzzle

Materials needed
Jigsaw puzzle of the United Kingdom.

Ask the children to complete a jigsaw puzzle of the United Kingdom. You will find that you can purchase these from commercial suppliers if they are not available in your school. Can the children identify the country which they live in? Where is your own village or town? What is the nearest feature shown on the jigsaw? Extend the activity using **Copymaster 2.17** (UK Jigsaw).

Activity 2.43: Borders

Materials needed
Map of the United Kingdom.

Talk about the boundaries of your school. How do you know where the school grounds finish and other land begins? Organise a walk around the edges of the site. What different types of border can you see? Get the children to record their observations on **Copymaster 2.18** (Borders), either working on their own or with the help of an adult. Look at a map of your country when you return to the classroom. In what places does the sea make a border? Where does the border cross the land?

Activity 2.44: Imaginary map

Ask the children to draw a map of an island divided into two different countries. The border might run along a river, cross a narrow neck of land or follow a mountain range. Talk with the children about the differences between the two countries. Can they think up names for them? Which one would they prefer to live in?

Activity 2.45: World map

Materials needed
A globe or map of the world that marks different countries.

Show the children a globe or map of the world. How are the different countries shown? What shapes can they see? Are some countries bigger than others? Where is the United Kingdom? What colour is the sea? Have any

children in the class ever been abroad? Ask them to find any countries that they have visited.

Activity 2.46: Stamps

Materials needed
Stamp collection from a number of different countries.

Put a selection of stamps from different countries out on display in the classroom. Can the children work out which country each stamp comes from? Ask the children to sort them into sets, using labels for the different countries. Do they have any stamps at home that they could contribute to the display?

Activity 2.47: Capital cities

Materials needed
Map of Europe or the world.

Talk about capital cities with the children. What makes them special? What is the capital city of your own country? Look at a map of Europe or the world. Get the children to identify some different capital cities. How many have they heard of before? Have any of the children visited a capital city?

Copymasters

2.15 Which Country? The children should colour the sea and the country that they live in, and tick the correct sentence at the bottom of the sheet.

2.16 Acrostic The children should write the words from the top of the page in the box that has the same initial letter. The sheet could easily be adapted to feature Wales, Scotland or Ireland. You might also ask the children to use place names of their own choice instead of the words on the sheet.

2.17 UK Jigsaw This copymaster provides children with a simple jigsaw. They should colour their own country and the sea, cut the sheet into four and see if they can put the pieces together in the correct positions.

2.18 Borders This is a survey sheet for use on a walk around the school grounds. The children should tick each different type of border as they find it.

NAME COUNTRIES OF THE UNITED KINGDOM

Area of Study 6

CM 2.19 –2.23

Statement of Attainment

Level 2

2a) Pupils should be able to name the countries of the United Kingdom.

Example and links with the Programme of Study

The children should know that their own country is part of the United Kingdom, which is made up of England, Wales, Scotland and Northern Ireland.

Introduction

The United Kingdom is a political unit. It is made up of England, Wales, Scotland and Northern Ireland. The United Kingdom has developed over a long period of time. The last major step in the process was the Irish Treaty of 1921, when Northern Ireland was formed.

This Statement of Attainment will raise questions about the features that distinguish a nation. With infants it is best to focus on visible clues such as the monarchy, national flag and capital city. Maps and atlases will be a valuable source of information.

In teaching this Statement of Attainment you need to distinguish between the United Kingdom and the British Isles. As both terms are in common use some children may question the difference. The British Isles are a physical, not a political, unit and this is the term used for the group of islands which lie off the north-west coast of the European mainland. They are Great Britain (England, Scotland and Wales), Ireland, the Orkney and Shetland Islands, the Isle of Man, the Scilly Isles, the Isle of Wight and the Channel Islands.

Key vocabulary

country	Scotland
England	United Kingdom
flag	Union Jack
Northern Ireland	Wales

Key questions

What are the differences between the countries of the United Kingdom?
In what way are they similar?

What sources of information can we use to find out about the United Kingdom?
How is the United Kingdom linked together?

Activity 2.48: The British Isles

Materials needed
Map of the British Isles.

Look at a map of the British Isles with the children. Explain that the British Isles consist of lots of different islands. Encourage the children to identify key features on the map such as the rivers, lakes and mountains. Help them to locate their own position on the map.

Activity 2.49: Different countries

Materials needed
Flash cards, map of the United Kingdom, drawing pins.

Make up some flash cards with the names of the different countries of the United Kingdom written in capitals and small letters. Get the children to place them at the correct point on a map of the United Kingdom. How can they tell where one country ends and another begins? Which of the four parts of the United Kingdom is the largest? Which part is the smallest? Reinforce this activity using **Copymaster 2.19** (The United Kingdom). You could also show them how the names appear in context using **Copymaster 2.20** (Names).

Activity 2.50: Countries snap

Materials needed
Light card, felt tips.

Scotland

England

Northern Ireland

Wales

Cards for 'Countries snap'

Make some playing cards based on the names and outline shapes of the countries of the United Kingdom. You will need eight cards in each set – four for the names and four for the shapes. Put several sets together to make a pack of cards and get the children to use them for games of snap. You could help to prepare the children for the game using **Copymaster 2.21** (Different Shapes).

Activity 2.51: Different flags

Materials needed
Map of the United Kingdom, gardening sticks, glue/Sellotape, scissors, plasticine.

Get the children to make flags for the different countries of the United Kingdom. **Copymasters 2.22 and 2.23** (Flags 1 and 2) provide outlines for the children to colour. They should cut these out and fix them to short poles made from gardening sticks. Lay out a map of the United Kingdom on the floor or some other horizontal surface and ask the children to plant the flags on the countries where they belong. A small lump of Plasticine makes a solid base and will stop the flags from falling over.

Activity 2.52: The Union Jack

Materials needed
A collection of items decorated with the Union Jack.

Explain to the class that the Union Jack is a combination of the flags of the different countries of the United Kingdom. Set up a display table with items that are decorated with the Union Jack. Examples might include tea towels, mugs, tins, pencils and other souvenirs. Encourage the children to contribute to the display. Discuss where you might see the Union Jack flying in your local area. When is it used?

Activity 2.53: Connections

Materials needed
Map of the United Kingdom.

Ask the children if they have any friends or relatives who live in a different part of the United Kingdom. Can they find where they live on a map? What country do they live in? Ask them to describe what it is like there. Is it crowded or empty, flat or hilly? Are there any important differences which the children can remember noticing?

Activity 2.54: Impressions

Materials needed
Large labels for the four parts of the United Kingdom, drawing pins.

Divide a display board into four sections, one for each part of the United Kingdom. Pin a label at the top of each section and ask the children to collect items for a class display. For example, the section on Scotland might include photographs of mountains and castles from magazines and calendars, tartan wrapping paper and a drawing of a Scotsman playing the bagpipes.

Activity 2.55: Countries game

Materials needed
Large labels, Sellotape, music.

Make large labels for each of the parts of the United Kingdom and put them up in the corners of the school hall before beginning a movement lesson. When the class is ready, play the children some music and ask them to dance. Every so often you should stop the music and call out the name of a country. The children then have to run to the correct corner. You can make the game more atmospheric by putting up flags as well

Different flags

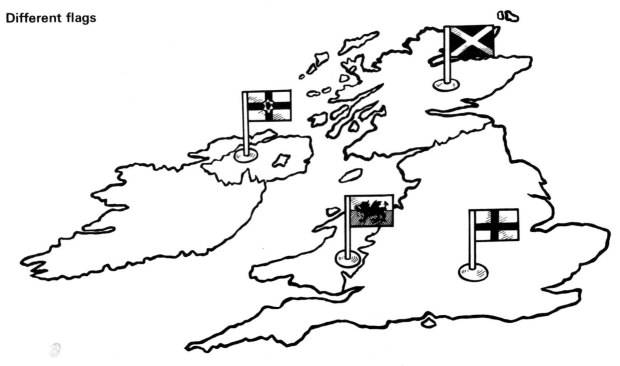

as labels, and playing appropriate pieces of music such as the bagpipes (Scotland), harp music (Wales), Morris dances (England) and Ulster marching songs (Northern Ireland).

Activity 2.56: Twister

Materials needed
Card, felt tips, paper fastener, Sellotape.

Join two large sheets of card together to make a Twister board. This should be divided into four equal sections, with the names of each part of the United Kingdom written in the middle of the four sections. You will also need to make a spinner. This should be exactly the same as the board but much smaller and with a marker in the middle that spins. Invite four children to play the game. One turns the spinner. The other three have to touch the board as directed. On the first go, the spinner tells them where to put their left

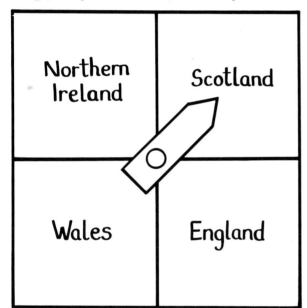

hand. On the second go the spinner tells them where to put their right foot, and so on. The players have to hold their positions. If they fall over or get the instructions wrong they are out of the game. The winner is the last person left.

Activity 2.57: Voices

Materials needed
Tape recorder, cassette.

Make up a tape recording of people speaking in the accent of their country. You might know people from different parts of the United Kingdom whom you could record speaking live. Alternatively, you might be able to find suitable cassettes in the local library. Play the cassette to the children and see if they can identify the accents. Extend the activity by reading the children stories and folk tales from different areas. Try to choose examples which capture the atmosphere of the place concerned.

Copymasters

2.19 The United Kingdom The children should colour the four parts of the United Kingdom and complete the labels.

2.20 Names The children should colour the picture and circle all the names of the parts of the United Kingdom they can find.

2.21 Different Shapes The outline shapes of the four parts of the United Kingdom are highlighted in this copymaster. Children should draw lines or arrows from the labels to the correct country.

2.22 and 2.23 Flags (1 and 2) The children should colour the drawings of the flags, cut them out, attach them to sticks and stand them upright on a map using a Plasticine base.

 Area of Study 7 | # DESCRIBE LOCAL LAND USE | CM 2.24 –2.26

Level 2 ▷ **Statement of Attainment**

2b) Pupils should be able to describe uses of land and buildings in the local area.

Example and links with the Programme of Study
The children should talk about the way land is used for homes, shops, farms, transport, recreation and industry. They should also consider different buildings in the local area.

Introduction
The way that people have used and altered their surroundings is of central concern to geographers. Human beings have had an immense impact on the

environment. Land-use studies can help to reveal this process and show underlying trends and patterns.

This Statement of Attainment introduces children to the idea of land use by looking at the examples in the local area. It builds on work done in Level 1 of this Attainment Target, in which pupils were asked to 'name familiar features' (Statement 1a).

It is important to start with small-scale examples. Most children will need to make studies in the class-room and school building before they are able to tackle

Children pin labels to
the correct part of the plan

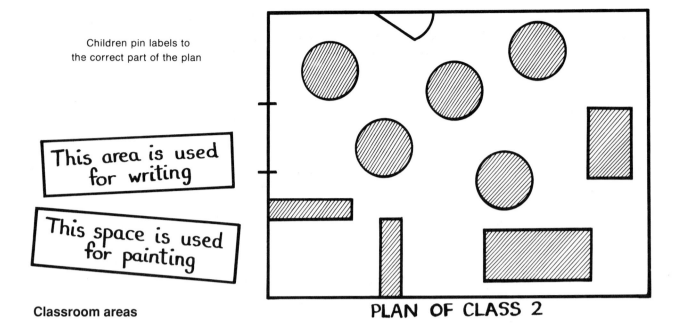

This area is used
for writing

This space is used
for painting

PLAN OF CLASS 2

Classroom areas

outdoor work. When they have acquired appropriate vocabulary and have developed a concept of area, they will then be able to look at local streets and buildings. It may also be possible to set up simple investigations for the children to work on.

Key vocabulary

bank	park
building	path
car park	place
church	post office
classroom	road
factory	school
house	shop
newsagent	street

Key questions

What are the different buildings and places in the local area?
How are they used?
Which things take up very little space?
Which things take up a lot of space?

Picture books

Many of the books mentioned under AT1 1b), 2e) and AT2 1a) will be relevant to this Statement of Attainment. Older children may also enjoy *The Mice and the Clock-work Bus* by Rodney Peppe (Penguin, 1986), which introduces the idea of transport in a light-hearted way.

Rhymes

This Little Puffin by Elizabeth Mattersen (Puffin, 1969) is a useful source.

Songs

Depending on your locality, there will be a variety of songs to choose from. For studies of the urban environment, 'Sing a Song of People' and 'Tower Block' from *Songs from Play School*, (Black, 1987) are particularly relevant.

Activity 2.58: Classroom areas

Materials needed
Large-scale plan of the classroom, labels, drawing pins.

Make a large-scale plan of the classroom and pin it on to the wall. Talk about the plan with the children. Can they identify the doors and windows? Where is their table or desk? Give the children labels describing how different areas are used. For example, one label might say 'This space is used for painting', and another might say 'This is where we keep our books'. Ask the children to pin the labels on to the correct part of the plan. Which things seem to take up the most space? Which things only need a small area? Are there any surprises or unexpected conclusions?

Activity 2.59: Areas in school

Materials needed
Large-scale plan of the school, labels, drawing pins.

Working in groups, go on a short walk around your school. Visit a number of different places. Ask the children what they are used for. Make a master list when you return to the classroom and get the children to pin labels on to a plan in the same way as they did for Activity 2.58.

Activity 2.60: School walk

Materials needed
Clipboards, paper.

Plan a walk around the school to visit all the different areas. Equip the children with clipboards, paper and pencils. As they go round they should note down how each place is used on a simple data collection sheet (see opposite page). Alternatively, you could get them to count up the number of different areas using **Copymaster 2.24** (School Walk).

PLACE	WHAT IS IT USED FOR?
Staffroom	Teachers relax here
Corridor	People walk along here

Activity 2.61: Different places

Materials needed
Camera and film, card labels.

Take a number of photographs of buildings and places in the vicinity of the school. Make a pair of labels to go with each photograph. The first label should describe the place, the second label should indicate how it is used. For example, a picture of the local church would need a label giving its name and a label saying 'prayers, weddings, and other church services'. Ask the children to match the photographs with the labels. It may help if you use different-coloured card for the different types of label. You can reinforce this work with **Copymaster 2.25** (Different Places), in which children link places with the way they are used.

Activity 2.62: Selling things

Talk with the children about the different places you can go to to buy things in the immediate neighbourhood. Can they name some of the shops? What are the things they can buy there? Make a visit to a local shopping precinct or shopping street. Collect information about the different shops using **Copymaster 2.26** (Shop Survey). Discuss the findings with the children when you return to school. Are there any shops which you would like to see set up in the area? Are any shops closing down? Can the children think of any changes to the shops?

Activity 2.63: Making things

Materials needed
Large-scale Ordnance Survey map of the local area, clipboards, pencils, paper.

Are there any places near your school where goods are made? Do any of the children have parents who work in local factories? What do they do? Look at a large-scale Ordnance Survey map of your area. Can the children identify the different places of work? Arrange a walk to visit some of them, and ask the children to make sketches to show what they look like.

Activity 2.64: Games and pastimes

Materials needed
General artwork materials.

Discuss the different places where the children go to play. Where are the nearest play areas, parks and sports centres? Are there any pieces of open ground which the children use unofficially? Ask the children to make a painting of a place where they play for a wall display. Get them to write a description underneath saying where it is, how it is used and whether the facilities are adequate (for example, 'There are lots of swings'.)

Activity 2.65: Roads

Materials needed
Large-scale Ordnance Survey map of the local area, camera and film.

Nearly a third of the land in towns and cities is taken up by roads and car parks. How many can you find on an Ordnance Survey map of your area? Working with the children, make a list of alleyways, cul-de-sacs, streets, paths, cycle tracks and dual carriageways near your school. Plan a walk that links together a range of different examples. Visit them with the children and take photographs to show what they look like for a class display.

Different places. Take photographs of different buildings and places.

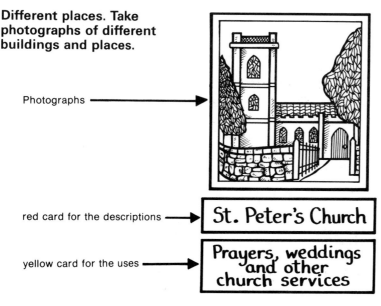

Photographs

red card for the descriptions → St. Peter's Church

yellow card for the uses → Prayers, weddings and other church services

Riverside Gardens

Playing games, picnics and relaxing

69

Copymasters

2.24 School Walk The children should complete this copymaster as they walk round the school. They could tick or colour the boxes as they find each example.

2.25 Different Places This copymaster will help children to consider how different places are used.

They should draw a line linking each place with the correct description on the opposite side of the page.

2.26 Shop Survey Use this copymaster in conjunction with Activity 2.62 (Selling Things). The children should record each shop they find by putting a tick in the correct box. When they return to school they could colour the boxes they have ticked to create a simple bar chart.

Area of Study 8

A CONTRASTING LOCALITY

CM 2.27 –2.33

Level 2

Statement of Attainment

2c) Pupils should be able to identify features of a locality outside the local area and suggest how these might affect the lives of the people who live there.

Example and links with the Programme of Study
The children should talk about places outside the local area by looking at postcards, photographs and other images. They should discuss features such as the weather, landscape, natural resources and type of settlement, and consider the impact that they have on everyday life.

Introduction
The relationship between people and the environment stands at the heart of geography. Housing, diet, clothing, employment and living conditions are all influenced by the physical surroundings. This Statement of Attainment directs attention to the way people respond to their surroundings.

Teachers are given a free hand to select any locality they like for the children to investigate. However, the Programme of Study for Key Stage 1 specifies that at some point pupils must study a contrasting locality in the United Kingdom. It makes good sense to combine the two requirements and to tackle them together.

When they study a contrasting locality, the children will need detailed information about everyday life there. It may prove possible to set up a link with a school in another part of the country and to exchange letters, tapes, photographs and maps. Alternatively, you could base the work on materials that you have assembled yourself, perhaps during a holiday or when visiting friends and relatives.

You should also bear in mind that contrasting localities can often be found within a short distance. Children in a suburban school, for example, could study a nearby farm or village. In large conurbations you might compare one urban area with another. In this way it is possible to make the best use of the environment and the resources that are available locally.

Key vocabulary

bank	harbour
boat	historic
bridge	kiosk
caravan	mine
castle	quarry
city	site
contrast	toilet
difference	tourist
farm	town
fishing	village

Key questions
What is the place like?
How does it differ from your own place?
What are the natural things in the area?
How have people changed the area?

Picture books
Some picture books have a strong regional flavour, or may be relevant to a particular locality. *A Walk in the Park* by Anthony Browne (Hamilton, 1977) is a case in point. With older children it may be appropriate to consider how the environment is changing. For example, *Shaker Lane* by Alice and Martin Provensen (Penguin, 1987) is about the effect of a new reservoir on an established community.

Activity 2.66: Contrasts

Materials needed
Pictures, photographs and maps of a contrasting locality.

Talk with the children about the features of the local area. What are the buildings and places which make it

Farm visit. The children can conduct their own interviews.

special? Now find out about a constrasting locality by looking at pictures, photographs, maps and other sources of information. In what way is it different from the place where you live? Record some of the key differences using **Copymaster 2.27** (Contrasts).

Activity 2.67: Farm visit

Materials needed

Clipboards, paper, pencils, tape recorder, camera and film.

Arrange a visit to a farm and talk to the farmer about the work there. What animals do they keep? How are these animals useful? Are there any crops? How many people work on the farm? It is best to get the children to prepare their questions beforehand. As well as writing down the answers, you might tape record the interview and take photographs of the things that you see. **Copymaster 2.28** (Farm) could be used either for preparation or for follow-up work.

Activity 2.68: Village visit

Materials needed

Photographs and map of a village or small settlement, camera and film.

Make a study of a village or small settlement. As well as looking at photographs you should provide the children with a map of the area. What are the key buildings? Make a class list. Plan a visit that will enable the children to see these different places. Get them to make field sketches and put them up as a class display when you return to school, **Copymaster 2.29** (Village) gives some idea of the things which the children could investigate.

Activity 2.69: Fishing port

Materials needed

Maps, brochures, slides and souvenirs of a fishing port.

Provide the children with information about a fishing port. This might be somewhere you have visited on holiday. Alternatively, you could arrange for someone you know to describe a port to the children in an illustrated talk. How many fishing boats are there, and what fish do they catch? Is the place popular with visitors? Is there a natural harbour? Do storms cause damage in the winter? **Copymaster 2.30** (Fishing Port) will help to develop key vocabulary as well as setting the scene.

Slides are an excellent way of conveying geographical information.

71

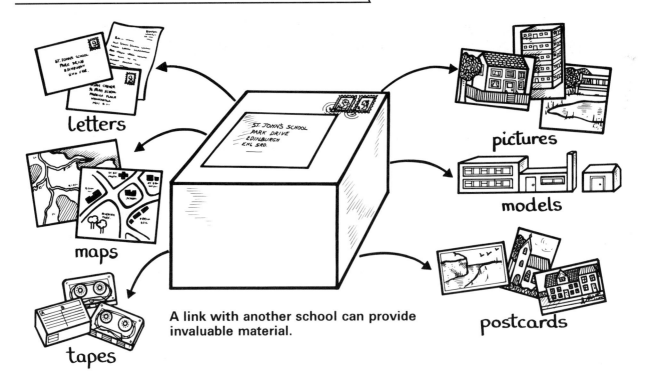

letters

maps

tapes

pictures

models

postcards

A link with another school can provide invaluable material.

Activity 2.70: Mining community

Materials needed

Leaflets and samples from a mining company. Maps and photographs of the surrounding area.

Write to a quarry or mining company for information about the work that they do. Enquire if they can send you a few samples of their products, along with pictures and brochures of their operations. Set up a display for the children to investigate. What is the name of the stone? What is it used for? How is it extracted? Put up a map of the mine and photographs of the places where the mine workers live. Talk with the children about the district. Any first-hand knowledge that you can contribute will be extremely valuable. Use **Copymaster 2.31** (Quarry) to support the work.

Activity 2.71: Tourist attraction

Materials needed

Tourist brochures and leaflets about a historic site, photographs, postcards and maps of the surrounding area.

Obtain brochures, leaflets and other promotional material about a tourist attraction such as an old abbey or castle. Where is it in relation to your own locality? Who lived there in the past, and why? How many people visit it nowadays? Provide the children with maps, postcards and photographs so that they can form an impression of the area. What clues are there that tourism is important for local people? As in Activity 2.70 (Mining Community), your own personal knowledge will be important when the children come to make their investigations. **Copymaster 2.32** (Historic Site) provides some ideas which the children can pursue.

Activity 2.72: School link

Materials needed

Letters, maps, pictures, photographs, cassettes, models and other materials from a school in a contrasting area.

Set up a link with a school in a contrasting area. Arrange for them to send letters, maps, pictures, photographs, cassettes, models and other materials which convey an impression of their locality. Using this evidence, get the children to set up a display that highlights the contrast with the place where you live. You might ask the children a set of questions to help focus their attention. It will also be valuable to consider why places develop in different ways. The interplay between human and physical geography will then become apparent. **Copymaster 2.33** (City) illustrates some of the features of a city environment and is designed to provide background information and vocabulary.

Copymasters

2.27 Contrasts The children should tick the first column to show the features in their own area and tick the second column to show features from a contrasting locality. This will help to highlight the diferences.

2.28 Farm, 2.29 Village, 2.30 Fishing Port, 2.31 Quarry, 2.32 Historic Site, 2.33 City. These copymasters are intended to support studies of a contrasting locality. The children should colour and label the pictures. They could also cut them out and use them in a picture of their own design. Alternatively, you might assemble the sheets as a frieze to illustrate the differences between localities in various parts of the United Kingdom.

COMPARE LOCALITIES

CM 2.34 –2.36

Statement of Attainment

Level 2

2d) Pupils should be able to describe the similarities and differences between the local area and another locality specified in the programme of study.

Example and links with the Programme of Study

The children should compare the local area with a contrasting locality in the United Kingdom or a locality beyond the United Kingdom. They should identify similarities and differences in farming, weather conditions, plants, animals, scenery, buildings, transport and people's lives.

Introduction

Case studies of specific locations illustrate how different geographical forces interact. This Statement of Attainment requires children to make a detailed appraisal of a particular place. Although the place could be anywhere outside the local area, there is much to recommend an overseas example. As well as showing significant differences, this will also satisfy the requirement for children to study a locality beyond the United Kingdom during Key Stage 1.

In order to make comparisons, children need to be familiar with their own locality. They will have gained knowledge of their surroundings when undertaking Statement 2b) of this Attainment Target, 'describe uses of land and buildings in the local area'. Some work on physical geography (Attainment Target 3) will also be essential preparation. It is important to remember that most of the information about an overseas locality will come from secondary sources. The children will therefore need to be practised in using interpretation skills.

Similarities and differences are best revealed by thinking in terms of geographical categories. The topics you could investigate include landforms, weather conditions, plants and animals, buildings, transport and work. If possible, the study should involve named people and families. There will also be opportunities to use maps to present and record information. In this way children will be able to build up an integrated picture of a place beyond their immediate experience.

Key vocabulary

animal	plants
area	scenery
buildings	similar
community	symbols
country	transport
different	weather
house	work
objects	world
place	

Key questions

What are the key features of the place where you live?
What are the key features of the locality you are studying?
In what ways is this locality similar to your own?
In what ways is it different?

Picture books

The similarities and differences between places is a theme which is explored in some modern picture books. *Jyoti's Journey* by Helen Ganley (André Deutsch, 1986) tells the story of an Indian girl who comes to live in England. *A Country Far Away* by Nigel Gray (Andersen, 1988) compares the life of a child in Africa with the life of a child in England.

Activity 2.73: Contrasting photographs

Materials needed
A collection of contrasting photographs.

Make a collection of contrasting photographs. These could show a variety of landscapes, buildings, types of transport, styles of dress, and so on. Ask the children to sort the photographs into groups. What differences do they notice between the pictures? Where do they think the pictures might have been taken? What clues help to tell them? As well as helping children to develop interpretation skills, this activity will introduce them to the idea of similarities and differences.

Activity 2.74: Matching descriptions

Materials needed
A collection of contrasting photographs and matching descriptions.

Devise short descriptions for each of the photographs used in Activity 2.73. Write them out on pieces of card and see if the children can match the descriptions with the photographs. Put them up as a display, and ask the children to add other examples, using photographs or drawings of their own.

Activity 2.75: Looking at pictures

Materials needed
Photograph, picture or poster of an overseas location.

Looking at pictures. Which features are similar and different to your own area?

Make a detailed study of a photograph or poster of an overseas location. Talk with the children about what they can see, and how this compares with your own area. Pay particular attention to landforms, weather, plants and animals, buildings, transport and people at work. Write a list of the things that the children mention and put it up on the wall next to the picture, using the headings 'similar' and 'different'. You could ask the children to complete **Copymaster 2.34** (Looking at Pictures) and **Copymaster 2.35** (Similar or Different?).

Activity 2.76: Symbols

Materials needed
Pictures or photographs of different places.

Put up some pictures or photographs of your locality and places overseas as a part of a wall display. Ask the children to colour and cut out the symbols in **Copymaster 2.36** (Symbols). They should then select the correct symbols for each picture and pin them underneath to complete the display. Talk about the

pictures. In what ways is your own area different from other places? In what ways is it similar?

Activity 2.77: Objects

Materials needed
Collection of objects from a locality overseas, photographs and books about the place chosen.

Talk with the children about the objects which give an impression of our lives. Make a list of a dozen key things. These should include clothes, toys, household objects, books and magazines. Now set up a display of objects from a locality overseas. You might obtain these yourself when on holiday. Another option is to set up a link with a school overseas, perhaps with the help of a local Development Education Group. Let the children sort the objects into groups and guess how they are used. What does each object indicate about the place that it comes from? Is it similar to or different from the things that we use? Get the children to make careful drawings of the objects. Books and reference material will help the children to find out more about the place where the objects originate.

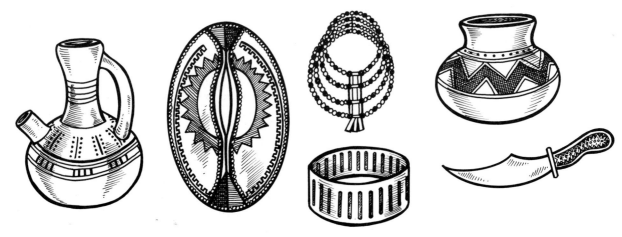

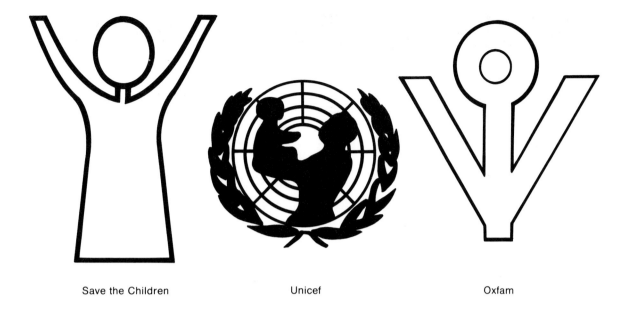

Save the Children   Unicef   Oxfam

Activity 2.78: Twinning

Materials needed
Maps, brochures and photographs of your twin town.

Find out from the local council if the place where you live is twinned with a community overseas. Many British towns have special associations with similar towns in France or Germany. See if you can arrange to borrow maps, brochures and photographs showing what your twin town is like. Is there anyone locally who has visited the place recently and who could give the children a first-hand account? See if it is possible to establish contact with a school in the area and to exchange information in a 'pen-pal' link. Organise a class project to explore the main similarities and differences. This could involve a great deal of cross-curricular work.

Activity 2.79: Overseas communities
Are there any children in the class who were born abroad? Ask them to talk about their country of origin. What clothes do they wear there? What food do they eat? What are their houses like? Can they bring in books, pictures and objects for the class to look at? You may find that one of their parents is prepared to come and help with the project. Alternatively, there may be other teachers or helpers in the school who can contribute. Get the children to make drawings, listen to music, play games and perform simple dances illustrating aspects of the culture of the place they are studying.

Activity 2.80: Television programme

Materials needed
Schools' television programme about an overseas locality.

Show the children a schools' television programme about an overseas locality. Since the introduction of the National Curriculum there has been an increasing number of programmes that provide portraits of life abroad. Use the programme as a stimulus for further work. For example, you might ask the children to make drawings and pictures for a concertina book about the place in the programme. You might also be able to broaden out the study to include more general information about the life and customs of the country.

Activity 2.81: Posters, packs and videos

Materials needed
Study packs from the main aid agencies.

Look at the publications lists from the main aid agencies, such as Oxfam and Save the Children. There are many new materials which have been produced to meet the requirements of the National Curriculum and to provide children with information about overseas localities. Use these as a starting point for a special project. You may find that you can incorporate them with Activities 2.77–2.80. Most of the packs, however, are extremely comprehensive and contain enough information for an independent study should other sources fail.

Copymasters

2.34 Looking at Pictures The children should complete this copymaster by studying a picture of an overseas locality and making lists or doing drawings in the empty boxes.

2.35 Similar or Different? This copymaster provides a drawing of a desert settlement. The children should consider each of the features listed and colour the circles to show if they are similar to or different from the place where they live.

2.36 Symbols The children should colour the symbols, cut them out and make a wall display by pinning the correct symbol under pictures of different places.

WORKING TOWARDS LEVEL 3

Programme of Study	Questions
Pupils should be taught to identify on globes or maps the points of reference specified on Maps A and C at the end of the programmes of study.	Where are the main mountains, rivers, seas and cities in the British Isles?
	Where are the main mountains, rivers, oceans, cities and countries in the world?
	What are the names of the continents?
Pupils should be taught to locate on a map the constituent countries of the United Kingdom.	What is the shape of the different countries of the United Kingdom?
	What are the boundaries between them?
Pupils should be taught to mark on a map of the British Isles approximately where they live.	What features help you to locate your position on a map?
Pupils should be taught to use correct geographical vocabulary to identify types of landscape features and industrial and leisure activities which they have observed in the local area.	What geographical words describe different landscape features?
	What geographical words describe different industrial activities?
	What geographical words describe different leisure activities?
Pupils should be taught to explain where economic activities are located in the local area and offer reasons for the location of specified activities in the local area.	Where are the main factories in your area? Are they near any major roads?
	Where are the secondary schools and hospitals? Are they on the edge of the built-up area?
	Where are the offices? Are they in a central location?
Pupils should be taught to describe the features and occupations of other localities studied and compare them with those of the local area.	Are there any mountains, rivers or lakes?
	What are the main settlements?
	Are there any harbours, airports, motorways or mainline railways?
	Where do people work?
Pupils should be taught to observe and suggest reasons for the relationships between land use, buildings and human activities in the local area.	Where are the shops in your area? Are they all easy to reach?
	Where are the factories? Are they scattered about or grouped together?
	Where are the farms? What crops do they produce?

76

ATTAINMENT TARGET 3: PHYSICAL GEOGRAPHY

Pupils should demonstrate their increasing knowledge and understanding of:

i)   weather and climate (the atmosphere);
ii) rivers, river basins, seas and oceans (the hydrosphere);
iii) landforms (the lithosphere); and
iv) animals, plants and soils (the biosphere).

Programme of Study for Key Stage 1 (Levels 1 & 2 only. For Level 3 see p. 87)

Physical geography

Pupils should be taught to:

- investigate soil, water and rocks, including sand, and recognise that these materials are part of the natural environment;
- identify water in different forms;
- identify familiar landscape features, including rivers, hills, ponds and woods, and explore different gradients of slope;
- investigate the effects of weather on themselves and their surroundings and recognise seasonal weather patterns.

ABOUT THIS ATTAINMENT TARGET ▶

The physical world is the context in which we live our lives. We all experience the weather, have contact with rocks and soils and make use of water in our everyday lives. This Attainment Target takes a close look at the physical environment and extends the children's experience in a structured way.

There is much here to excite young children. Distant locations such as deserts, forests and icecaps can capture the imagination. Stories of journeys and adventures introduce a personal and human dimension. Some parts of the world are still almost unknown, and the exploration of space is one of the most exciting frontiers of modern knowledge.

There are good opportunities for cross-curricular work. Topics such as 'water' and 'weather' are ideal for introducing the main ideas and concepts. The links with the science curriculum are particularly strong. Mathematics and English are also involved.

Fieldwork and practical activities are a good way of approaching these studies. Opportunities will vary depending on the nature of the locality. The seashore, woodlands and hills can be used to illustrate many key ideas. In urban areas the landscape is often obscured by buildings but the features become apparent in river-banks, parks and other areas of open space. If you have established your own resource bank of photographs and pictures then this will be useful. There are a number of infant 'big books' and other publications which also provide valuable reference material on landscapes, weather and seasons.

BACKGROUND INFORMATION FOR THE TEACHER ▶

The earth is one of nine planets which orbit the sun. It takes the earth $365\frac{1}{4}$ days to revolve round the sun, which is approximately 150 million kilometres away. Venus and Mars are our nearest neighbours.

Origins of the earth

We do not know how the earth was formed, but scientists believe it began as a swirling cloud of gas and dust some 4600 million years ago. Unlike other planets, the earth has plenty of water and a dense atmosphere which is rich in oxygen. This has made it possible for life to develop.

The earth's crust

Nearly 70 per cent of the earth's surface is covered by water. Land occupies the other 30 per cent. Much of the land is uninhabitable as it consists of deserts, mountains and ice. In the remaining areas the soil and weather conditions enable people to grow crops.

The outer surface of the earth is known as the crust. This varies in thickness from five to 70 kilometres. Beneath the crust there is a zone of molten and semi-molten rock called the mantle, and a core which is made of iron. Very little is known about either of them.

Landforms

Geographers have always been interested in the processes which affect the earth's surface. They study the different landforms and the way they have been created. They investigate rocks, and compare climates. They attempt to account for the distribution of animals, plants and soils. These different elements are the key components of physical geography.

Planet Earth

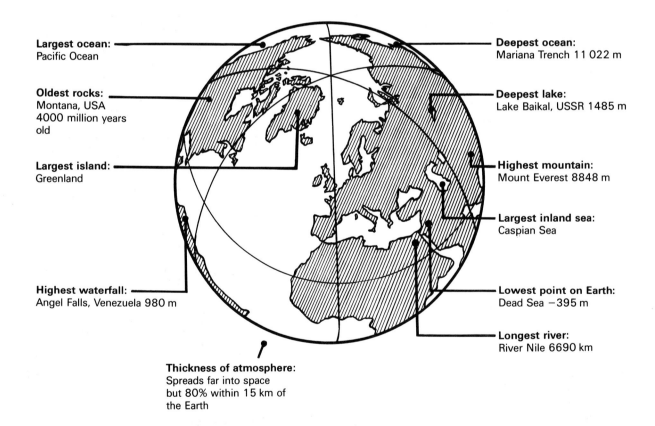

Largest ocean: Pacific Ocean

Oldest rocks: Montana, USA 4000 million years old

Largest island: Greenland

Highest waterfall: Angel Falls, Venezuela 980 m

Thickness of atmosphere: Spreads far into space but 80% within 15 km of the Earth

Deepest ocean: Mariana Trench 11 022 m

Deepest lake: Lake Baikal, USSR 1485 m

Highest mountain: Mount Everest 8848 m

Largest inland sea: Caspian Sea

Lowest point on Earth: Dead Sea −395 m

Longest river: River Nile 6690 km

Facts and figures

● Distance around the equator: 40 000 km.

● Distance to the centre of the Earth: 12 700 km.

● Temperature at the centre of the Earth: 4500°C.

● Distance to the moon: 384 000 km.

● Distance to the sun: 150 000 000 km.

● Distance to the nearest star: four light years.

ROCK, SOIL AND WATER

CM 3.1 –3.5

Statement of Attainment

Level **1**

1a) Pupils should be able to recognise rocks, soil and water and understand that they are part of the environment.

Example and links with the Programme of Study

Children should be able to tell the difference between rock, soil and water. They need to be able to discriminate between liquids and solids, understand that solids can be hard or soft and know that they occur in different ways in the natural environment. They should also know that sand is a type of rock.

Introduction

Rocks, soil and water are the elements which make up the earth's crust. Together with the atmosphere they form the environment in which we live. It has taken many millions of years for the earth to evolve into its present state. The coming together of the elements which support life must have been a rare chance. Astronomers have not yet discovered another similar planet in the universe.

Young children will be familiar with rocks as pebbles and stones, they will have played with sand, soil and water and know some of their main characteristics. This Statement of Attainment aims to build on children's tactile experiences. It will help children to recognise different materials in the environment and to sort them into geographical categories.

Key vocabulary

chalk	puddle
clay	rock
earth	sand
fossil	sea
pebble	soil
plant	stone
pond	water

Key questions

What are the differences between rock, soil and water?
Where are they found?
What lives in them?
How do they affect our lives?

Songs

'The Wise Man and the Foolish Man' (*Okki-Tokki-Unga*, edited by B. Harrop, Black, 1976) highlights the difference between rock and sand in a way that young children can readily understand.

Activity 3.1: Rock collection

Materials needed

Rock collection, magnifying glass, binocular microscope, reference books.

Set up a collection of unusual rocks and stones. Try to include some fossils and a variety of different colours and textures. Get the children to contribute by bringing in their own examples. Have a magnifying glass and, if possible, a binocular microscope to hand so that the children can examine the collection properly. As well as sorting the rocks into groups, the children might identify them in simple reference books and discuss where they come from.

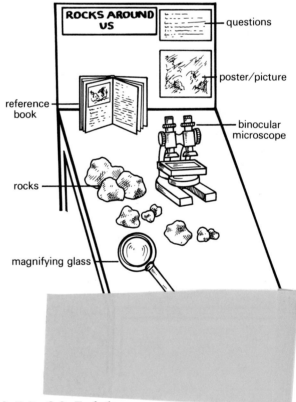

Activity 3.2: Feely box

Materials needed

Empty crisp boxes, margarine tubs, stones, soil.

Turn some empty crisp boxes into feely boxes. You will need an empty margarine tub for each one. Put a stone in the first box, some soil in the second and a small quantity of water in the third. Get the children to put their hands inside and describe what they find. Ask

detachable numbers (these can be moved round to make the game 'new' for each child)

BOX 1

What is in this box?

500 g margarine tub filled with rock, soil or water goes inside.

them to talk about whether the items are hot or cold, rough or smooth, sharp or round, soft or solid, and so on. After a while the children will get to know what the boxes contain, so it is a good idea to swap the tubs round or to change the numbers on top of the boxes. You could extend the work using **Copymaster 3.1** (Rock, Soil and Water).

Activity 3.3: Miniature garden

Materials needed
Seed tray or shallow wooden box, fast-growing seeds, moss, twigs.

Make a miniature garden with rocks, soil and earth in a seed tray or shallow wooden box. Group some of the stones together to make a rockery or high point. Scoop out some of the earth to make a sunken or low point for water. Bring the garden to life by planting a few fast-growing seeds such as mustard and cress, and add some moss, twigs and other suitable items. The

children will need to discuss where to put them, and should create a realistic arrangement. They could record what they have made using a simple picture map.

Activity 3.4: Looking at sand

Materials needed
Some small trays of sand, plastic buckets, tubes and pots, simple play equipment.

Find out about the characteristics of sand. Let the children play with buckets, tubes and pots using dry sand. Does the sand flow smoothly and evenly? What happens when the sand is mixed with water? Get the children to describe what it feels like. What different models can they make? You could set up an experiment to see what happens when sand dries out. Ask the children to make some castles from wet sand. Get them to label when the castles were made and see what happens to them as they dry out. Use **Copymaster 3.2** (Sand Castles) to record the results.

Activity 3.5: Different soils

Materials needed
Samples of different types of soil, jars or transparent bottles.

Collect samples of soil from different places around the school or neighbourhood. Try to include gritty soil, clay, dust, and so on. Return any living creatures that you find so that they are not disturbed. Use the soil samples for some simple experiments. Can the soil be rolled into a ball like Plasticine? What are the differences in colour between the samples? What happens when the soil is mixed with water? Get the children to make a display of jars or bottles so they can see how the soil samples settle after they have been mixed and shaken with water (see illustration).

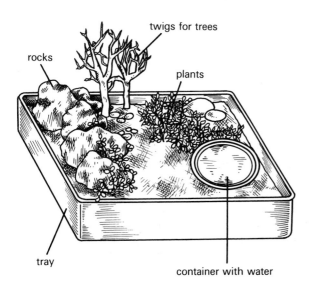

twigs for trees

rocks

plants

tray

container with water

Gritty soil   Fine soil   Mixed soil

Different soils. Study soil samples from different places around the school.

Activity 3.6: Different surfaces

Materials needed
Toy vehicles, trays of soil and sand.

Get the children to bring some toy vehicles to school. Find two trays or shallow containers. Fill one with sand and the other with soil. Ask the children to experiment with these different surfaces. Can they build a road for their toy vehicle? Which is better – sand or soil? Why are streets covered with tarmac? Do builders use any other materials to make roads strong?

Activity 3.7: Investigating the school grounds

Materials needed
Plastic bottles, margarine tubs with lids, plastic bags.

Look for different examples of rocks, soil and water in the school grounds. You could take some containers with you for collecting what you discover. Use plastic bags for pebbles and stones, margarine tubs for soil and plastic bottles for water from puddles. Bring what you have collected back to the class and set up a display. Add labels saying where each item came from.

Activity 3.8: At the park
Make a visit to a nearby park to see how the soil has been used in flower beds, grassy slopes and play areas. Look at the way rocks are made into rockeries, paths and walls. You might also find there is a pond, boating lake or fountain you can look at. **Copymaster 3.3** (At the Park I Spy) will help the children to record information. It can be used on site with the help of an adult, or completed back at school from memory.

Activity 3.9: Rocks in buildings
Arrange a visit to a local building made of stone. You might select your local church, a municipal building or perhaps a castle or ruin. Look at the ways that stone is used. Get the children to copy any patterns or carving that they see. Discuss where the stone might have come from. Why are so few buildings made of stone nowadays?

Activity 3.10: Seashore visit
Arrange a visit to the seashore. If possible, choose a place where children can work safely among rock pools. Look for plants and creatures which have made their homes on the rocks, in the water and on the sand. You will find that **Copymaster 3.4** (The Seashore), and **Copymaster 3.5** (Seashore I Spy) both help to develop the work and reinforce the children's experience.

Copymasters

3.1 Rock, Soil and Water   This sheet establishes the differences between rock, soil and water. The children should colour the drawings and draw lines linking each drawing to the correct word in the middle of the page.

3.2 Sand Castles   Children should use this copymaster to record what happens to their sand castle as it dries out.

3.3 At the Park I Spy   This survey sheet will help children to record the things they see in the park. They should tick each item as they find it. Back at school they might colour the drawings to show what they discovered.

3.4 The Seashore   The drawing on this copymaster illustrates how rock, soil and water are combined in the physical environment. When the children have completed the work you could get them to colour the picture and arrange the sheets as a class display, perhaps with a lighthouse at the centre of the display.

3.5 Seashore I Spy   This sheet should be used to record a seashore visit. It concentrates on the plants and creatures that live in different places. As in the previous 'I Spy' sheet, children should tick the boxes to show what they have discovered.

81

WEATHER AND SEASONS

CM 3.6
–3.9

Level 2	Statement of Attainment
	2a) Pupils should be able to recognise seasonal weather patterns.

Example and links with the Programme of Study

Children should observe the weather and record their experiences using appropriate vocabulary and artwork techniques. They should also be taught the differences between the seasons and be able to recognise seasonal clues.

Introduction

There are considerable variations in weather conditions around the world. Sunshine, wind, rain and snow all combine in different ways. In the United Kingdom the weather changes within hours and people take great interest in weather forecasts. Four seasons of roughly equal length –spring, summer, autumn, winter – mark out the year. Each has its own characteristic features.

The seasons give a rhythm to our lives. Even the youngest children are aware of winter snowfall, summer holidays and the growth of plants in spring. School terms and festivals like Christmas and Easter help to emphasise the pattern. This means that there are plenty of opportunities for relating a study of the seasons to the children's own understanding and enthusiasm.

Key vocabulary

autumn	shower
cloud	snow
cold	spring
dry	summer
fog	water
frost	weather
hot	wet
rain	wind
season	winter

Key questions

What season is it now?
What clues tell you about the season?
What is the weather like today?
Is the weather the same as yesterday's?
What would help you guess tomorrow's weather?

Legends

The weather and seasons often feature in traditional tales and legends. The story of Demeter and Persephone can be found in many anthologies of Greek myths. You might also explore links with other cultures in countries such as India and China, and the Caribbean.

Picture books

There are a number of popular picture books which illustrate the impact of weather on our lives. *The Weather Cat* by Helen Cresswell (Collins, 1989) is a good example. It is a charming story about a cat that can forecast the weather.

Poems

Most poetry anthologies contain poems about the seasons and weather. *This Little Puffin* edited by Elizabeth Matterson (Puffin, 1969) has a whole section on weather games. *A Calendar of Poems* by Wes Magee (Collins, 1986) is another useful source.

Songs

One of the best sources for songs about the seasons is *Every Colour Under the Sun* by Redvers Brandling (Black, 1983). Songs such as 'Summer's Really Here' are an ideal way of consolidating work based on this Statement of Attainment.

Activity 3.11: Dressed for the season

Materials needed

Dressing-up clothes, old cardboard boxes.

Divide the clothes in the dressing-up corner into seasonal collections. One way of doing this is to set up four large cardboard boxes, one for each season. Get the children to label the boxes and draw pictures on the front. They can then play at dressing up for different times of the year, while other members of the class guess which season they have chosen. Winter and summer are easy to distinguish but autumn and spring will be much less clear-cut. In our climate each season can have a wide variety of weather. Extend the work using **Copymaster 3.7** (The Right Clothes).

Activity 3.12: Musical moods

Materials needed

Tapes or records of seasonal music.

Many pieces of music evoke the seasons. One of the most famous is Vivaldi's *The Four Seasons*, but there are also many modern examples. Plan an assembly using seasonal music and songs. You might find that some of the traditional stories and myths provide a structure. Many of them seek to explain the forces of nature in human terms.

Season tree. Make a collage of seasonal changes.

Activity 3.13: Season tree

Materials needed

Cotton wool, tissue paper, paints and crayons, scissors, glue.

Make a picture of four large outline trees for a class display. Get the children to complete each one as a seasonal collage. Add blossom for the spring, green leaves for the summer, falling leaves in yellow and brown for the autumn and put snow on the branches for winter.

Activity 3.14: Seasonal words

Put the names of the seasons as headings on a display board. Get the children to write out all the weather words they can think of and pin them under the headings where they think they belong. Discuss the reasons for their choices. Add other words to do with seasonal activities. Think about the life cycles of plants and animals. How do the seasons affect what we do and the clothes we wear?

Activity 3.15: Poetry box

Materials needed

Light card, scissors, glue.

Working as a class, make a list of words to describe the current season. Use these as the starting point for a poetry lesson. There is no need to make the poems complicated. A few contrasting words and phrases can convey the character of a season with great effect. You could extend the work by asking the children to write a different poem for each season. They could then decorate the poems and glue them on to a strip of card to make an open box. This creates an attractive table decoration which the children can take home to show their parents.

Poetry box. Get the children to write short seasonal poems.

Activity 3.16: Seasonal Cluedo
Here is a list of clues for spring and autumn.

Spring	Autumn
Blossom	Storms
Tadpoles	Falling leaves
Lambs	Conkers
Daffodils	Bonfires
Cuckoos	Harvest
Sowing seeds	Berries
Birds' nests	Toadstools
Buds and leaves	Dew
Showers	

Write each of these clues on a piece of card. It would be helpful if you could add drawings or pictures to go with each one. Arrange the classroom with two large tables opposite each other and a large space for the children to sit in the middle. Put a label 'Spring Clues' on one of the tables and label the other one 'Autumn Clues'. You might put a child in charge of each table and give them a special spring or autumn hat.

Place the cards on the floor and get the children to read them out one at a time. The class should then discuss which table they think each card should be placed on. When the game has finished the children can record the words on **Copymaster 3.8** (Spring and

Autumn Clues). To extend the game the children could decide on clues for winter and summer in the same way.

Copymasters

3.6 Snap Cards   Get the children to work in pairs for this activity, and check that they know how to play snap. Before they begin they will need to colour the cards and cut them out. It helps if you can reproduce the copymaster on light card for durability.

3.7 The Right Clothes   This sheet could be used as a free-standing exercise, or to support a project on clothes. The children cut out the pictures and rearrange them in the right order. They will need card, glue and scissors to do the work.

3.8 Spring and Autumn Clues   This sheet is designed to be used in conjunction with Activity 3.16, Seasonal Cluedo. Children should write or draw the clues in the empty spaces. A similar recording sheet could be used for summer and winter clues.

3.9 Season Dial   The aim of this activity is to link the seasons with the months of the year. It could be used at any point in a project on the seasons and links well with work on time and calendars.

WATER IN THE ENVIRONMENT

CM 3.10/
–3.13

Area of
Study
3

Statement of Attainment

Level
2

2b) Pupils should be able to identify the forms in which water occurs in the environment.

Examples and links with the Programme of Study
Children should know that water occurs in the environment as rain, fog, clouds, ponds, rivers and seas; and that it freezes to create ice, hail, frost and snow. They also need to be aware of the effects of water on the landscape as it runs down slopes.

Introduction
Geographers are particularly interested in water because it covers so much of the earth's surface. The processes of evaporation, condensation and precipitation account for the development of weather systems. Rivers and glaciers shape the landscape as they wear away rocks. All living creatures depend on water for their survival.

Water is a familiar part of children's lives. Not only is it essential for health and hygiene, it also features in many games and pastimes. Seaside holidays are especially popular, and many children enjoy playing in pools and puddles. It may surprise them to learn that water commonly occurs in the environment in three

very different forms – liquid, gas and solid. The opportunities for links with science are particularly strong in this Attainment Target.

Key vocabulary
cloud	rain
drizzle	river
flood	sea
fog	slope
frost	snow
hail	steam
ice	water
lake	waterfall
pond	

Key questions
Where does water come from?
Does water run uphill?
How does water disappear from puddles?
Does ice always melt?
How do we use water?
What would we do without it?

Legends

Floods feature in many myths and legends. The most obvious is perhaps the story of Noah, which provides a good link with religious education.

Stories

There are a number of children's stories which deal with the effect of water on the environment. 'In Which Piglet is Entirely Surrounded by Water' from *The House at Pooh Corner* by A.A. Milne (Methuen, 1928) is a particularly good example and introduces a wide variety of geographical vocabulary.

Songs

Harlequin by David Gadsby and Beatrice Harrop (Black, 1981) is a rich source of songs about water. 'Snowflakes', 'Ho! Jack Frost', 'The Umbrella Man' and 'The Rain Song' are just some of the songs which pick up the idea of water in the environment.

Activity 3.17: Water experiments

Materials needed

Plastic cups, jugs, bottles, water wheel and other play equipment, Plasticine, sand trays, watering can, watering can roses.

Fill a number of different containers with water. Does water have a special shape? Pour it down a tube onto a wheel. What happens? Does water always flow downhill? Working in a suitable part of the school grounds, pour water from a watering can to create 'raindrops'. See what happens when you change the watering can rose. Where does the water go as it reaches the ground? Are there any streams or miniature lakes? Try to create a dam and lake in a sand tray.

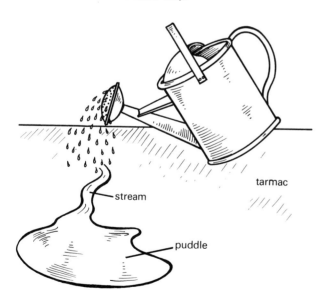

Activity 3.18: Frozen water

Materials needed

Ice cubes, saucers or dishes.

Bring some ice cubes to school in an insulated container. Set up an experiment with the children to find out how quickly they will melt. Put the cubes on saucers in different places around the classroom. Do they all melt at the same time? What has caused them to melt? Leave the saucers out for a period of a few days. Get the children to note any changes in the water level. Where is the water going? Record the experiment using **Copymaster 3.10** (Frozen Water). Talk about places in the world where the ice cubes would not have melted.

Activity 3.19: Word mobile

Materials needed

Card, scissors, coat hanger or gardening sticks, thread or string.

Make a mobile of water words. Write the words on pieces of card and arrange them in three groups: vapour words – fog, mist, cloud, steam; liquid words – rain, pond, river, sea; solid words – ice, hail, snow, frost. Suspend them from a coat hanger or frame made of gardening sticks, using thread or light string. You could add a two-dimensional globe to the centre of the mobile to emphasise that all the words describe the physical environment.

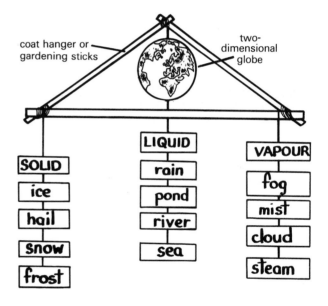

Activity 3.20: Water walk

Go for a water walk around your school to discover all the different things which are to do with water. Examples might include drainpipes, taps, drains, drinking fountains and puddles. Get the children to note down what they discover, either using **Copymaster 3.12** (Water Survey) or by making simple labelled sketches.

Activity 3.21: Playground quiz

Materials needed

Outline plan of the school playground.

Take the children into the playground and decide:
1 The best place to shelter from the rain.
2 The best place to see a pond or puddle.

3 The best place to make a slide in winter.
4 The best place to see flowing water.
5 The best place to see the most clouds.

Get the children to help you mark these different places on an outline plan while you are outside. Back in the classroom, the children should then write a few sentences about the places they have visited and pin their descriptions to the correct part of the plan.

Activity 3.22: Water and landscapes

Materials needed

Outline drawing and materials for class collage, photographs of different landscapes.

Make a large landscape collage showing water in lots of different forms. It could include clouds, streams, lakes, rivers, ponds, reservoirs, waterfalls and the sea. Get the children to write labels and pin them to the correct part of the collage. You might find it helpful to discuss photographs of different natural landscapes in order to develop their vocabulary. You could also reinforce the work by using the words for syllable clapping in music or associated language lessons such as poetry.

Activity 3.23: Adventure story

Read the children an adventure story about a journey to a distant land. This might involve crossing oceans, fording rivers, travelling through woods and forests or over mountains. *Percy Short and Cuthbert* by Susie Jenkin Pearce (Viking, 1990) is a good example. See if the children can draw a picture map to show the route taken. Make up a similar story with the children. Draw a map showing the route and naming some of the main landmarks. **Copymaster 3.13** (Sun and Showers) could be used to illustrate the idea of a story sequence.

Copymasters

3.10 Frozen Water This sheet is intended to help children record the results of the ice cube experiment. It introduces the idea of a flow diagram in its simplest form.

3.11 Rain or Snow? The effect of temperature on water is explored in this activity sheet. The question of how we measure temperature should be discussed before the children complete it.

3.12 Water Survey The children should tick one box in the grid panels for each item they discover. There is an empty space in the bottom right-hand corner for the children to draw any other items they notice.

3.13 Sun and Showers A sunny morning is sometimes followed by a showery afternoon and a dry evening. This copymaster introduces the idea of sequence. Children should colour the pictures, cut them out and glue them down on a separate piece of paper in the right order.

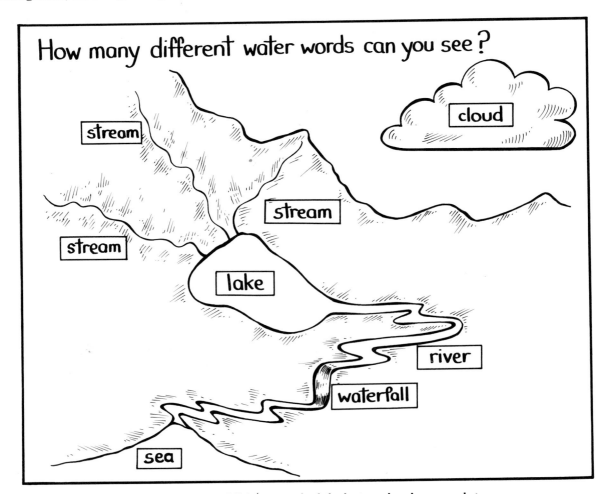

Water and landscapes. Get the children to pin labels to a landscape picture.

WORKING TOWARDS LEVEL 3 ▶

Programme of Study	School-based work	Contrasting locality	World dimension
Pupils should be taught to identify and describe landscape features, for example, a river, hill, valley, lake, beach, with which they are familiar.	What are the high and low places in your school? What landscape features can you see through the classroom window? What are the main features of the school site?	What landscape features do you find in the mountains? What landscape features are found on the coast? Which landscapes do you like most?	What are the world's highest mountains? What are the world's biggest oceans? What are the world's longest rivers?
Pupils should be taught the effect of different surfaces and slopes on rainwater when it reaches the ground.	Where does water run to when it rains? Where do puddles form? Which places dry out quickly after rain, which stay wet? Why?	How are homes constructed to keep out the rain? In what ways are marshes special? What are the main rivers of the United Kingdom?	Which places suffer from floods? How do people deal with floods? What are the world's biggest waterfalls?
Pupils should be taught about weather conditions in different parts of the world, for example, in polar, temperate, tropical desert and tropical rainforest regions.	Which are the warmest and coldest parts of your school? What types of weather are you having today? Is it cold or hot, wet or dry?	What differences in weather are there in the United Kingdom? (Use yesterday's weather map.) What is the highest and lowest temperature recorded in the United Kingdom?	Which places are always cold? Which places are always dry? Which places are always hot and wet?

ATTAINMENT TARGET 4: HUMAN GEOGRAPHY

Pupils should demonstrate their increasing knowledge and understanding of:

i)   population;
ii) settlements;
iii) communications and movements; and
iv) economic activities - primary, secondary and tertiary.

Programme of Study for Key Stage 1 (Levels 1 & 2 only. For Level 3 see p. 110)

Human geography

Pupils should be taught:

- to investigate the uses made of buildings in the local area and further afield;

- to investigate how people make journeys, why different means of transport are needed and why people make journeys of different lengths;

- that most homes are part of a settlement and that settlements vary in size;

- how goods and services needed by the community are provided;

- that adults do different work, *for example, a teacher, bricklayer, bus driver, nurse, voluntary worker, a person looking after a housebound relative.*

ABOUT THIS ATTAINMENT TARGET

This Attainment Target considers different aspects of human activity. It involves the study of people and the places where they live. It also considers the way people travel from one place to another, and how they earn a living. These are huge topics, as the working group which devised the National Curriculum admitted from the very beginning.

The strand headings are particularly helpful in drawing attention to the main areas of study. Population, settlement, communication and economic activities are themes which recur at many different levels.

Infants are not expected to become deeply involved in these issues. The curriculum requires them to find out about just three elements – buildings, journeys and work. These are things which can be studied using the child's own experience. There are also good opportunities for fieldwork and practical activities.

One of the challenges in teaching children about the everyday world is that the subject matter seems so ordinary. Yet, by looking in detail at the local environment, children can discover a wealth of geographical interest. Simple observation naturally leads to more complex enquiries. Even something as ordinary as a door handle, for example, raises questions about the use of resources, historical change and social attitudes.

Most studies of human geography are easy to link up with other areas of the curriculum. Cross-curricular themes to do with environmental education, health and industry can be explored through integrated topics. The focus on people also makes a natural bridge to the humanities, especially history and English. This should be considered in the planning done by the whole school when devising suitable schemes of work.

BACKGROUND INFORMATION FOR THE TEACHER ▶

Young children are growing up in a world of constant and increasing change. The problems of population growth and environmental pressures are paramount. It is important that we introduce children to these issues so that they can begin to understand current events. Some key points are briefly outlined below.

Population
The world is currently facing an unprecedented population explosion. In 1900 there were approximately 1600 million people. By the year 2000 this figure will have increased approximately fourfold to 6000 million.

Settlement
Many countries are in the throes of an urban revolution. Over half the world's population will soon be living in towns and cities. Nowhere is the pace of change faster than in the developing world. This is precisely the area which has the least resources to cope.

Communication and movement
In recent years there have been major advances in transport technology. Air routes, for example, now link places that were previously inaccessible. This means that in many respects the world is becoming steadily smaller. Modern electronic communication systems have reinforced this trend. All countries now belong to a world economic order, and different markets and industries depend on each other for economic health and prosperity.

Economic activities
In the United Kingdom and other parts of Western Europe the old industrial centres have given way to new electronic industries and the service sector. It is often no longer possible to identify centres of production. Most cars, for example, are assembled from components that come from several different countries. At the same time, structural unemployment, where workers are offered only short-term contracts of employment and then laid off, has become a fact of life, and many people have moved into new forms of work such as self-employment.

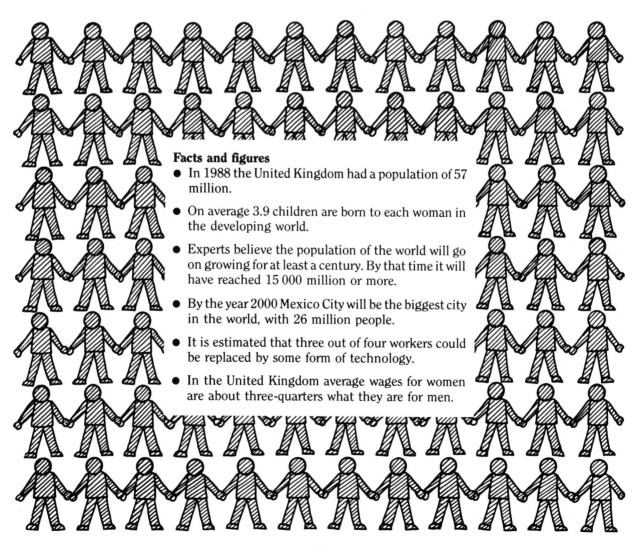

Facts and figures
- In 1988 the United Kingdom had a population of 57 million.

- On average 3.9 children are born to each woman in the developing world.

- Experts believe the population of the world will go on growing for at least a century. By that time it will have reached 15 000 million or more.

- By the year 2000 Mexico City will be the biggest city in the world, with 26 million people.

- It is estimated that three out of four workers could be replaced by some form of technology.

- In the United Kingdom average wages for women are about three-quarters what they are for men.

USES OF DIFFERENT BUILDINGS

CM 4.1 – 4.4

Area of Study 1

Level

1

Statement of Attainment

1a) Pupils should be able to recognise that buildings are used for different purposes.

Example and links with the Programme of Study

Children should consider a range of buildings which are familiar to them, and talk about the uses of homes, shops, offices, factories, schools and places of worship in the local area and further afield.

Introduction

Villages, towns and cities are composed of buildings. One of the best ways of finding out about a settlement is to study the different buildings which make it up. This Statement of Attainment directs attention to the local environment but also involves the study of settlements in more distant locations.

All buildings are a response to human needs. Homes provide us with shelter, factories are designed so that people can work together, while churches cater for our spiritual life. The children should discuss these different uses of buildings. Ideally they should make visits to some of the key buildings in the locality and meet the people who use them. However, they will also need to work from secondary sources such as pictures and photographs. As always when working with young children, it is best not to take anything for granted. For instance, infants, being small in stature, may not see buildings as a whole but merely as walls and barriers.

Key vocabulary

buildings	greengrocer
butcher	home
café	office
castle	petrol station
cathedral	post office
church	railway station
factory	school
farm	shop
garage	

Key questions

What buildings do you find where you live?
What buildings might you find in the country?
What buildings might you find by the sea?
Why do shops, homes and factories need to be different?
Which buildings are most important?

Poems

There are a number of poems about houses in *This Little Puffin,* compiled by Elizabeth Matterson (Puffin, 1969).

Rhymes

There was an Old Woman

There was an old woman
Who lived in a shoe.
She had so many children
She didn't know what to do.
She gave them some broth
Without any bread,
And whipped them all soundly,
And put them to bed.

Here's the Church

Here's the church and here's the steeple,
Open the door and here are the people.
Here's the parson going upstairs,
And here he is a-saying his prayers.

(The children should mime each phrase with their hands.)

Activity 4.1: Different buildings

Materials needed

Selection of magazines, scissors.

Make a list of all the different buildings the children can think of. Examples might include houses, shops, offices, garages, churches, cinemas, and so on. Use **Copymaster 4.1** (Different Buildings) to help the children link the names of buildings with their pictures. Give the children some old magazines and ask them to cut out any pictures of buildings they discover. Put these up as a wall display under the headings *This is where we live, This is where we work, This is where we spend our spare time.*

Activity 4.2: Name the parts

Materials needed

Large cardboard cut-out of a house, labels for the different parts.

Make a large cardboard cut-out of a house. This could open out so that the children first see the doors and windows and then look into the rooms. Get the children to name the different parts of the building. Can they match the labels to the correct room or part?

Name the parts. Get the children to pin labels to a model of a house.

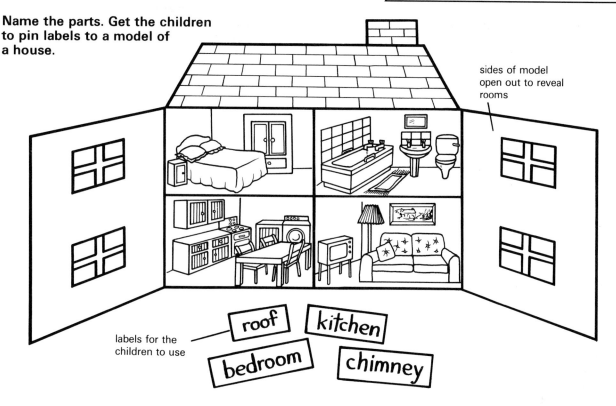

sides of model open out to reveal rooms

labels for the children to use

roof   kitchen   bedroom   chimney

What is each part of the house used for? Ask them to draw similar drawings of their own houses. They could include a picture of themselves in each of the rooms to help bring it to life. **Copymaster 4.2** (Houses) will reinforce the work and could provide an alternative way of teaching the same ideas if you do not have time to make a model.

Activity 4.3: Rooms with a purpose

Materials needed
Dolls' house, shoe boxes, pieces of wood, fabric and Plasticine.

Get the children to arrange the furniture and people in the dolls' house. See that there is a different activity going on in each room. Ask them to explain why they

put the things in the places they have chosen. To extend the activity, get the children to make a model of a room using an old shoe box. Small pieces of wood and fabric are ideal for making furniture. Plasticine can be used for smaller items and for modelling figures. When the children have completed the work, ask them to draw a simple plan or picture showing the arrangement they have created. This is a useful opportunity to introduce mapwork in context, and the children will already be very familiar with the layout of the objects.

Activity 4.4: Building quiz

Materials needed
Pictures or drawings of parts of different buildings.

Show the children a picture or drawing of one part of a building and ask them to guess what it is. You might

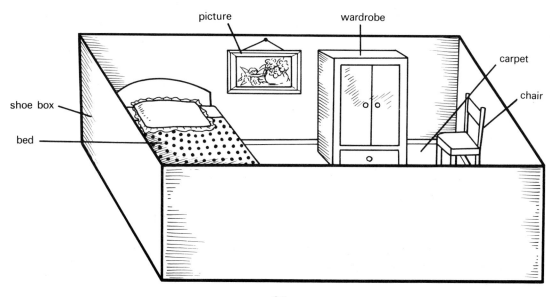

picture

wardrobe

carpet

chair

shoe box

bed

select the doors, roof, chimney or some other distinctive clue. Try to include a wide range of examples, such as castles, cathedrals, factories, power stations and oil rigs. Discuss what the buildings are used for and why they are needed. Let the children make up their own clues using pictures from magazines, then put them up in a class display and see if the rest of the class can identify what they come from.

Activity 4.5: Comparing buildings

Arrange a visit to two different buildings in your locality and talk to the people who work there about what they do. Perhaps the most obvious place to start is the local parish church. As well as being used for regular services, special services and events such as marriages, baptisms and concerts also take place there. Other buildings to visit might include a nearby shop, garage, railway station or office. **Copymaster 4.3** (Inside a Church) shows the interior of a parish church and is designed for children to colour, and as a prompt for discussion and language work.

Activity 4.6: Places of work

Materials needed
Photographs or pictures of people doing different indoor jobs.

Give the children photographs or pictures of people who work at different indoor jobs. These might include a nurse, a teacher, a librarian, a chef or a waitress. Ask the children to paint the place where each person works. Pin the pictures up as a class display and put labels under each one saying what it shows.

Activity 4.7: Building survey

Go for a short walk around your neighbourhood with your class. What different buildings can the children discover? Record the number of shops, churches, offices, factories, garages, petrol stations, and so on. **Copymaster 4.4** (Building Survey) provides a framework for the children to record the information. You might present the results of the survey as a simple pictogram. There are also opportunities for discussing your findings. Are there any conclusions you can draw about the pattern of buildings near your school?

Activity 4.8: Buildings around the world

Materials needed
Photographs or pictures of buildings in different countries.

Give the children a collection of photographs or pictures of buildings around the world. Get them to sort them into places for living, places for working, places for worship, and so on. Discuss the differences that the children notice. Would they like to live in these buildings or visit them? Can they explain why

they are different? Use the pictures on a number of different occasions, and get the children to sort them into sets using a variety of criteria, such as buildings from hot and cold lands, buildings for large and small numbers of people, buildings which look ugly and buildings which are attractive.

Activity 4.9: Fantasy houses

Materials needed
Crayons, paints and other artwork materials.

Read the children the rhyme about the old woman who lived in the shoe (see page 90). Discuss how she fitted all her family into such a small space. Where were the windows, chimney, front door, and garden? Get the children to do paintings to show the old woman's house. Extend the idea by thinking about other unusual houses. How could a flower pot, Wellington boot or kettle be turned into a home? Who might live there, and why?

Copymasters

4.1 Different Buildings   This copymaster is designed to introduce children to some basic types of buildings. As well as completing the labels, the children should colour the drawings.

4.2 Houses   This copymaster focuses on descriptive vocabulary and will encourage children to observe their immediate environment with greater care.

4.3 Inside a church   In most localities the church will probably be the most distinctive building. This colouring sheet should be used to prompt discussion, and as a way of extending the experience of a visit.

4.4 Building Survey   The children should tick one box in the grid panel for each building that they discover. You may want to provide them with a blank piece of paper for any buildings which are not shown on the survey sheet.

WAYS PEOPLE TRAVEL

CM 4.5 –4.10

Statement of Attainment

Level 1

1b) Pupils should be able to describe ways in which people make journeys.

Example and links with the Programme of Study

Children should describe the journeys they make to school by car, bus, bicycle, taxi, and on foot. They should also discuss and record how people make journeys of different lengths when they go shopping, see friends or travel to work.

Introduction

The journeys which people make and the way that they travel has always been of interest to geographers. In the past, most people travelled on foot or by animal. Nowadays, cars, buses, trains, boats and aeroplanes link many places together. Each major transport system has its own routes. The way that these inter-relate tells a complex and fascinating story.

This Statement of Attainment introduces children to the idea of communications. It also involves the idea of a journey, and raises questions about the means of transport. Many young children travel from place to place in the back of a car and sometimes gain little impression of the places that they visit. As a result they may have little direct experience of journeys which the teacher can develop.

The journey to school is a good starting point as it is something which children have to do on a daily basis. Discussing family journeys in the locality is a way of extending this idea. Holidays in distant locations and other countries introduce another dimension. You can also link this theme to suitable picture books and children's stories. Even if children have not travelled far in reality, it is always possible for them to make visits overseas in their imagination.

Key vocabulary

aeroplane	port
airport	railway
bicycle	road
boat	school
bus	ship
car	shop
country	station
distant	taxi
ferry	train
friends	walk
holiday	work
motorway	

Key questions

What do you see on your way to school?
What journeys are made by other members of your family?

What vehicles do they use?
What are the advantages and disadvantages of walking from place to place?
Why do people go on journeys?

Picture books

Children's stories often describe journeys. Examples include *Mr Gumpy's Motor Car* by John Burningham (Cape, 1973) and *The Riverboat Crew* by Andrew McLean (Oxford, 1978). Some journeys, such as the one in *Rosie's Walk* by Pat Hutchins (Bodley, 1968) also suggest a definite route which children can map.

Poems

Read the children 'The Owl and the Pussycat' by Edward Lear. How did the owl and the pussycat travel? What preparations did they make, and what happened to them?

Rhymes

One Big Tanker Goes Rolling By

One big tanker goes rolling by.
How many big wheels can you spy?

Two big tankers go rolling by.
How many big wheels can you spy?

Three big tankers go rolling by.
How many big wheels can you spy?

Four big tankers go rolling by.
How many big wheels can you spy?

Five big tankers go rolling by.
How many big wheels can you spy?

Songs

'The Train is A-Coming' from *Apusskidu* by Beatrice Harrop (Black, 1975) is a popular song.

Activity 4.10: Getting to school survey

Materials needed

Small pieces of card, glue, scissors.

Make a survey of how children in your class come to school. You could either get the children to draw symbols of their method of transport on a piece of card, or cut them out from **Copymaster 4.5** (Ways of Travelling). Arrange the symbols to create a pictogram. What form of transport is used most? Is there any reason for this? Get the children to consider the route

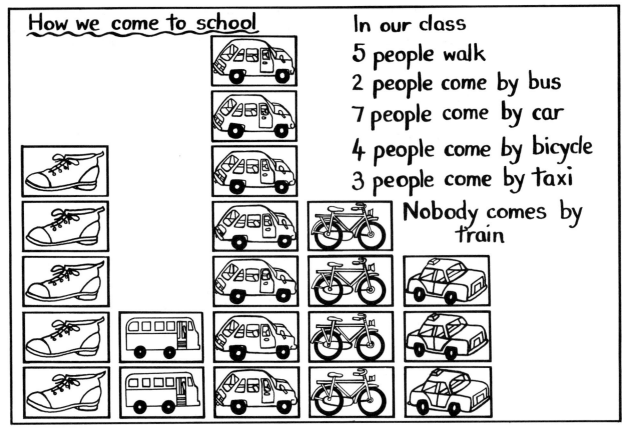

Getting to school survey

that they take. What are the obstacles that get in their way? Would it be quicker for them to come by any other means?

Activity 4.11: Toy vehicles

Materials needed

Toy vehicles, cardboard tubes, paper straws, cotton reels, small pieces of wood and other modelling equipment.

Set up a display of different toy vehicles and discuss how they are used. Get the children to arrange them on a display board as a traffic jam at a road junction. Ask them to bring some of their own toys from home to add to the collection. Can the children sort them into different groups, for example vehicles which carry people, vehicles which carry goods? Set them a challenge to design a vehicle that will carry a toy brick. You could provide a range of modelling equipment such as cardboard tubes, cotton reels, paper straws and small pieces of wood. Ask the children to talk about the problems they had to solve in making their model.

Activity 4.12: Bus journeys

Which of the children in the class have been on a bus? Discuss their journeys and list the places they went to. Use **Copymaster 4.6** (Bus Journeys) to make a class picture. You could put all the buses together to make a bus depot, or you could spread them out along a road. Ask the children to bring in bus timetables and old bus tickets. Are any of the children's parents or relatives

bus drivers or conductors? See if you can arrange for them to come and speak to the class about their work, the people they meet and the places they go to.

Activity 4.13: Transport survey

Go into the playground and make a survey of all the different vehicles that you see in a five-minute period. You might see cars, vans, lorries, bicycles, motorbikes and buses on the road, trains on nearby railway lines and aeroplanes in the sky. **Copymaster 4.7** (Transport Survey) will help you record the results. Which vehicles appear to be used most? Which vehicles are used least? It is interesting to repeat the survey at a different time of day to see if there are changes. You could also ask the children to think about vehicles which they know about but did not see. Examples might include ships, helicopters and underground trains.

Activity 4.14: Vehicle collage

Materials needed

Old magazines, scissors, glue.

Give the children some old magazines and ask them to cut out any pictures of vehicles that they discover. Put the pictures up on the wall as a collage. Get the children to add labels naming each vehicle and saying what it carries. Try to include a range of examples. For instance, if the children can find a picture of a cement mixer, a Post Office van or a horse box it will help to promote discussion. As an alternative, they might make their own drawings of some more unusual vehicles from books. **Copymaster 4.8** (Car Game) is one way of extending the work in a light-hearted manner.

Activity 4.15: Holiday journeys

Materials needed
Paper, string or wool, card, artwork materials.

Ask the children where they have been during the holidays and how they travelled there. This might involve a simple questionnaire which the children take home to complete with their parents. **Copymaster 4.9** (Holiday Journeys) is designed for this purpose. As not all children will go away for a holiday, emphasise that they might have made a short trip, such as to the park. Make a display of the information you have collected. Start by asking the children to draw a picture of themselves, and get them to write a sentence underneath saying where they went and how they travelled. You should then ask them to fix their drawing on to a display board. You can convey the idea of distance using three concentric rings. The first or inner ring will show destinations near to home, the middle ring destinations elsewhere in the United Kingdom, and the outer ring destinations abroad. Add lines of string or wool connecting each picture to the centre of the display and discuss any patterns that emerge. For example, did most of the children who visited places near to home travel by car? Did those who went abroad travel by plane?

Activity 4.16: Obstacles
Discuss the different obstacles people have to overcome when they make journeys. Bridges, viaducts and embankments help us to cross valleys. Cuttings and tunnels pierce mountains. Ferries and air services link places separated by the sea. Get the children to make drawings of some of these things or ask them to colour and complete **Copymaster 4.10** (Obstacles) by joining the dots.

Activity 4.17: Famous journeys
Talk to the children about famous journeys people have made. You might tell them about the attempts to climb Mount Everest, the exploration of the oceans, Scott's journey to the South Pole, or missions in space. Discuss the different methods of transport used. What special equipment was required? Get the children to draw their own vehicle for a special journey. How will it deal with the problems and obstacles on the route?

Activity 4.18: Stories of journeys
Get the children to talk about stories and poems that they know of which involve a journey. *Rosie's Walk* is a good example. Ask the children to make a map showing the different places that Rosie visits. Make sure that they add the names of some of the key features. Check carefully that the features are in the correct order. Could another child follow the map they have drawn?

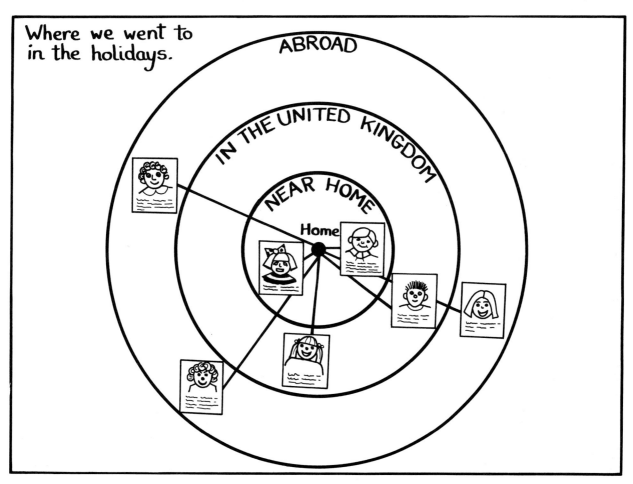

Copymasters

4.5 Ways of Travelling This copymaster provides symbols for a survey of how children travel to school. Get the children to colour the symbols and select one to show the method of transport that they use.

4.6 Bus Journeys Get the children to colour this sheet and write down where the bus might be going to. You can then use the finished drawings in a class display.

4.7 Transport Survey This sheet is intended to help children record the different vehicles that they see when they make a survey. They may need an adult to help them complete it.

4.8 Car Game The children should play this game in small groups. They throw the dice in turn and colour or tick the part of the car which corresponds to their number. The first child to complete their car is the winner.

4.9 Holiday Journeys The children should take this copymaster home and complete it with the help of their parents. Use the information from the surveys to complete Activity 4.15.

4.10 Obstacles The children create a route by joining the dots together. This illustrates how bridges, tunnels and other devices help to overcome obstacles.

CM 4.11 –4.14

DIFFERENT KINDS OF WORK

Area of Study 3

Level **1** ▷ **Statement of Attainment**

1c) Pupils should be able to recognise that adults do different kinds of work.

Example and links with the Programme of Study
The children should talk about the people they have seen working, and discuss what they do. Examples could include a teacher, bricklayer, bus driver, nurse, voluntary worker, and a person looking after a house-bound relative.

Introduction
There are many different types of employment. Some people work indoors, others work outside. Jobs can require physical strength or mental activity. Sometimes people work on their own, more frequently they form part of a team. This Statement of Attainment will already be familiar to many teachers. 'Work' has been a popular topic in infant schools in recent years, and there is a wealth of material that has been prepared for class use.

It is logical to begin by discussing the jobs which the children have witnessed directly. You could then consider different kinds of jobs, what people do and why they do it. The question of skills and qualifications might also be raised, together with the idea of payment. Do the children know anybody who works unusual hours or has to travel widely in their job? If you can, arrange for adults to visit the class bringing special equipment or materials which they need to do their job.

Key vocabulary

assistant	cook
bricklayer	dentist
bus driver	doctor
caretaker	factory

farm	secretary
helper	shift
holiday	shopkeeper
job	skill
nurse	teacher
office	work
postman	

Key questions
What is work?
What jobs do people do locally?
Can they be divided into categories?
Who organises them?

Picture books
The Postman Pat stories by John Cunliffe (published by André Deutsch and Hippo Books) have proved very popular with young children over the years, and help to introduce the idea of work. Postal services also feature in *Katie Morag Delivers the Mail* by Mairi Hedderwick (Bodley, 1984). It is worth noting that all the Katie Morag books are set on the Isle of Struay and have a picture map on the inside front cover.

Poems

The Policeman

The policeman walks with a heavy tread,
Left, right, left, right,
Swings his arms, holds up his head,
Left, right, left, right.

(Children mime as the words suggest.)

Soldiers

See the soldiers in the street,
Hear the marching of their feet;
They are singing as they go,
Marching, marching, to and fro.
See the soldiers in the street,
Hear the marching of their feet.

(Children march round separately in a long line to the tune of 'Twinkle, twinkle, little star'.)

Songs

Suitable songs include 'On a Work Day I Work' from *Every Colour Under the Sun* by Redvers Brandling (Black, 1983) and 'The Fireman' from *Apusskidu* by Beatrice Harrop (Black, 1975).

Activity 4.19: What is work?

Split the class into groups and give the children a range of activities and exercises to do. These might include number work, reading, modelling, painting, and so on. Get the children to change activities every 15 minutes so that they do a mixture of different things. At the end of the session get the children to discuss what they did. Which things were fun, which things were hard work? Were any activities particularly popular? Does work need to be unpleasant? How do we know when we are working?

Activity 4.20: Everyday jobs

Talk with the children about all the different people who help to run a school. Get them to think about the people that they don't always see, such as the dustmen and delivery drivers, as well as the teachers and other people that they meet. Invite the caretaker, cook or some other member of staff to come and talk about their job. What do they like and dislike about what they have to do? Do they need any special equipment or clothing? Get them to bring these things along with them for the children to look at.

Activity 4.21: People who help us

Discuss the different people who help the children in some way as part of their job. Examples might include nurses, doctors, the police, Post Office workers, shop assistants, and so on. Get the children to make paintings of these different people for a class display. They can make each person look different by showing the uniform that they wear or something distinctive that they use. Extend the work using **Copymaster 4.11** (Parcel Post). Consider the different jobs which are done at home. Are people always paid for the things they do? Can the children think of any volunteer or charity workers that they know of? Why do they not get paid?

Activity 4.22: A place of work

Arrange a visit to a place of work in your locality. A shop, supermarket or office might prove suitable. List the different jobs that people do. Get the children to make a sample study of just one occupation. They might ask a few simple questions using **Copymaster 4.12** (Job Questionnaire). What job would the children like to do when they are grown up? Get them to give reasons for their answers.

Activity 4.23: Car production line

Materials needed

Crayons or felt tips, scissors, glue, frieze paper.

Set up a simple car production line. You will need to divide the children into groups and get each group to produce a different part – the wheels, body or windows. **Copymaster 4.13** (Production Line) provides cut-outs for the children to use. See how many pieces the

PEOPLE WHO HELP US

milkman   nurse   policewoman   caretaker   doctor

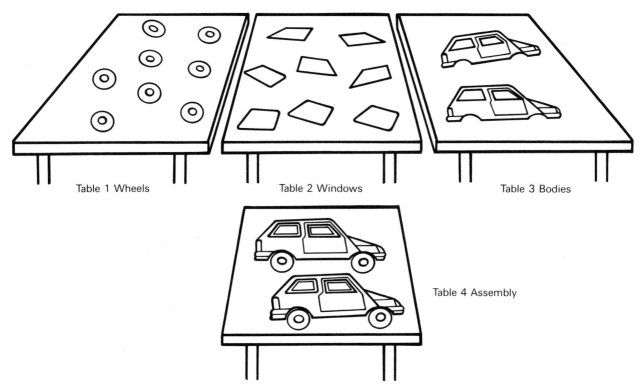

Table 1 Wheels   Table 2 Windows   Table 3 Bodies

Table 4 Assembly

The car production line

children can colour in a given time. Give other children the task of glueing the parts together. How many complete cars can be assembled? Mount them on frieze paper. What are the advantages of having a production line? Can the children think of any disadvantages?

Activity 4.24: Acting a job

Materials needed
Dressing-up clothes, a collection of workers' hats.

Turn the play corner into a shop, factory or some other place of work. Allow the children to choose the workplace and organise themselves. Then discuss the job each one is going to do. Have they remembered all the different workers? In a shop, for example, there might be a counter assistant, manager, shelf-filler, cleaner, delivery driver and health inspector. Encourage the children to take on a variety of different roles. One way of doing this is to provide them with a number of different hats. These are fairly easy to improvise and can be cut out of card. **Copymaster 4.14** (Different Hats) might help to stimulate ideas. Get the children to act out the different roles. Can other children guess what they are? Which role do they prefer, and why?

Activity 4.25: A dictionary of jobs

Materials needed
Pictures from magazines.

Working with the children, make a list of as many different jobs as possible. Can you find a job for every letter in the alphabet? Make up a dictionary of jobs as a

wall display. Get the children to write a sentence describing each one. Cut out a picture to illustrate each job from old magazines. If it proves impossible to find all the pictures you need, the children could do drawings instead.

A Dictionary of Jobs

A is for acrobat. Acrobats work at the circus.

B is for builder. Builders make houses.

Activity 4.26: Jobs around the world

Materials needed
Photographs and pictures of people around the world.

Collect and display photographs of people doing work in other parts of the world. These might include 'formal' work for an employer, 'informal' work in which people earn a living for themselves (for example, by cleaning shoes) and unpaid work (collecting water and firewood). The various aid agencies are a good source of teaching materials (see address list, page 132). Discuss why people do these different jobs. Is there any evidence that men and women do different work? How are jobs changing?

Activity 4.27: Job detective

Materials needed
Puzzle box containing a piece of wool, a milk bottle top, something made of wood, and other items.

Discuss with the children what the items in the box all have in common. The conclusion should be that they all come from the countryside. Discuss the jobs that might be involved in producing each material and distributing it. For example, the milk bottle top is part of a chain which involves the farmer, milk lorry driver, dairy worker, bottle maker, manager, milkman and cashier/accountant. The children could record some of these sequences by setting up a flow chart as a class display.

Activity 4.28: Music while you work

Sing some of the songs which people have invented to make their job easier and to pass the time in repetitive and physically-demanding work. Examples include 'Heigh Ho, It's off to work we go!' and sea shanties. Develop some of these ideas in movement lessons by getting some of the children to act out the different jobs – lifting the anchor, digging a trench, and so on. Can other children guess what it is they are doing?

Copymasters

4.11 Parcel Post This copymaster highlights the fact that postmen need to find their way round a great number of streets and buildings. Children should draw the route through the maze and colour the pictures.

4.12 Job Questionnaire Use this sheet to help collect information on a site visit or when somebody comes to your class to talk about their job.

4.13 Production Line You will need to cut this sheet into three parts and give each part to the appropriate group in the assembly line. It is best to make the copies on light card if possible.

4.14 Different Hats Hats are one of the simplest ways of conveying an impression. Get the children to colour the pictures and complete the sentences as a way of encouraging them to make hats of their own.

| Area of Study 4 | **HOMES AND SETTLEMENTS** | CM 4.15 –4.18 |

Level 2	**Statement of Attainment**
	2a) Pupils should be able to demonstrate an understanding that most homes are part of a settlement, and that settlements vary in size.

Example and links with the Programme of Study
The children should look at and talk about pictures, maps and photographs of homes in villages, towns and cities in different parts of the world.

Introduction
Geographers have always been interested in settlements, from isolated farms to large cities. They study the features of individual sites, compare different towns and villages, and try to account for their growth and evolution. This Statement of Attainment lays the foundation for these investigations by establishing the idea that settlements vary in size.

Young children need time to absorb this concept. They have a highly egocentric view of the world. Their home and other familiar environments are enhanced and enlarged in their imagination. More remote places, by contrast, merge into an undifferentiated haze.

One way of teaching this Statement of Attainment is by working outwards from familiar things. Using discussion, stories and the children's experience it will then be possible to build up a more complex image. Ultimately children should be led to consider settlements in other parts of the world, and the different homes which make them up.

Key vocabulary

building	cathedral
bungalow	church
castle	factory

flats
garage
garden
home
hotel
house
office

road
school
shop
station
street
town
village

Key questions

What type of settlement do you live in?
What are the special buildings that are found in villages?
What are the special buildings that are found in towns and cities?
What different types of houses are there?
Are settlements different in other parts of the world?

Folk tales

Towns and cities feature in many legends. 'The Pied Piper of Hamelin' and 'Dick Whittington' are two examples which give children a clear view of cities from the past.

Picture books

A Day in the City by Maria Ruis (Parramon, 1986) describes some of the different buildings found in towns.

Poems

This Little Puffin, compiled by Elizabeth Matterson (Puffin, 1969) has a whole section of poems about the things people see in towns.

Activity 4.29: Street survey

Materials needed
Ordnance Survey map of the locality.

Arrange a visit to a street near your school. Try to choose somewhere with a variety of buildings and give the children **Copymaster 4.15** (Street Survey) to help them record what they find. Back at school you could make a block graph showing the buildings in the street you visited. You might also look at a large-scale Ordnance Survey map. Can the children find the key buildings, such as the shops and the church? How many houses can they see? How can you tell the difference between buildings by looking at their plan?

Activity 4.30: Where we live

Materials needed
Ordnance Survey map of the locality, crayons, paper, string or wool.

When the children go home in the afternoon, ask them to take a careful look at their homes so that they can draw them the next day. Get them to look especially at the number on the door, the number of windows and the shape of the roof. Ask the children to make their drawings using crayons and paper. Arrange the pictures on the wall around a map of the locality. Join them to the correct place on the map using string or wool. Write underneath, *We live in a village/town/ city.* Complete **Copymaster 4.16** (Where I live) as a way of extending the work.

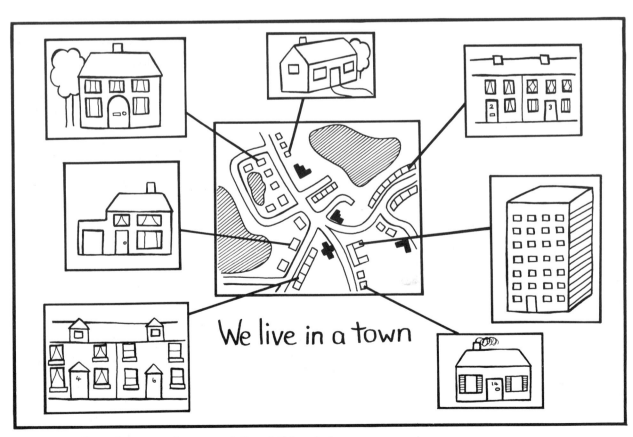

Where we live. Arrange pictures of the children's homes around a map.

Activity 4.31: Types of house

Materials needed
Pictures of houses, class scrap book.

Discuss with the children all the different types of homes that they know about. Examples will include houses that stand on their own, terraced houses, flats, bungalows, cottages, chalets, hotels, houseboats, cabins, summer houses, and so on. See if they can find an example of each one for a class scrap book. Write the name of the house underneath.

Activity 4.32: Making a settlement

Materials needed
Crayons, glue, large sheet of card for base of model.

Using **Copymaster 4.17** (Houses), get the children to make some house models. They will need to fold along the solid lines and glue down the flaps. It will help if you have made an example beforehand so that you can demonstrate it to the class. Arrange the first models that are completed on a base board to form a village. As more houses are added you can watch the village grow. This illustrates how settlements change. How many houses would be needed to turn the village into a small town? Get the children to agree on where the roads and other features might be found, and complete the model by gluing down the houses and adding a church and some shops.

Activity 4.33: Wall map

Materials needed
Large squares of card, felt tips, paints and artwork materials.

Make a map of the area around the school for a class display. Begin by cutting out some large squares of card and fixing them lightly to the wall to cover all the available space. Discuss with the children where to mark the school, streets and main landmarks. Draw these on the map with felt pen, and decide on a standard colour code. For example, you might use red for the roads, green for the parks and yellow for the houses. You can now remove the squares from the wall and give them to individuals or small groups to paint.

When the squares are reassembled the class will have made a base map of their locality. They can then begin to add drawings of houses and significant buildings such as the school and church, and add names of key places.

There are a number of different ways of developing the wall map idea. One approach is to ask the children to make collage pictures of the different buildings using pieces of coloured tissue paper. This can be most impressive to look at, but is very time-consuming. Another idea is to make each 'tile' or square into a relief model. If this is done in clay the sections can be fired and made into a permanent work of art.

Activity 4.34: Photograph album

Materials needed
Old and new photographs of your local area.

Make an album of photographs showing different views of your local area. This could show ordinary streets and houses as well as places of special interest. Invite an old age pensioner to come and talk about how the area has changed. See whether they have any photographs or postcards to compare with modern scenes. Make photocopies of these and add them to your collection. Find out about the history of your settlement. Did it start as a village and turn into a town? Is it somewhere that has been carefully planned, like a new town? Did it grow up as a suburb around a railway station?

Activity 4.35: Town model

Materials needed
Small cardboard boxes, cardboard tubes and cylinders.

Get the children to make buildings out of cardboard boxes. It will help if they work in small groups and keep to fairly simple shapes. Put the models together to make a town or village. Discuss the good and bad points about the scene they have created. You could extend the work by using tubes and cylinders to make a city. Use groups of cylinders of different heights to represent tower blocks and tall buildings in the city centre. Place some sideways to show low structures such as factories and industrial units.

  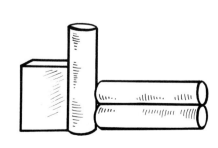

tower blocks   city centre   factory units

Town model. Use tubes and cylinders to create a town model.

Activity 4.36: Newspaper city

Materials needed

Strips of newsprint, glue, scissors, black sugar paper.

Impressive pictures of skylines can be made by arranging strips of newsprint on black sugar paper. The tallest strips will represent skyscrapers or blocks of flats. Other buildings, such as houses, factories and churches, can be suggested by cutting appropriate roof shapes. The children could add trees and clouds to finish the city. This could be completed as a class exercise and presented as a frieze. Alternatively, children could work on their own. It is important that you discuss the pictures. The proportion of houses to other buildings is a particularly vital point.

Activity 4.37: Paint a story

Materials needed

Paint, paper and brushes.

Select a story which involves a town or village. 'Dick Whittington' and 'The Pied Piper' are both good examples because they are particularly evocative. Discuss what the children think the places in the story might have looked like. Are the streets narrow or wide? Are the buildings tall and crowded, or low and well-spaced? What other buildings are there? Let the children make their own painting of the town or village, perhaps showing it from a distance. Finally, add a title or caption underneath.

Activity 4.38: Concertina book

Materials needed

Pictures and photographs of houses in different countries, card and Sellotape.

Make a collection of pictures of different homes and settlements around the world. You could provide some to start the project off, but the children should be encouraged to bring in their own examples from brochures, newspapers and colour supplements. Mount the pictures on pieces of card and fix them together to make a concertina book. The children will be excited by how the book grows, and the interest it provokes will provide a continual point of discussion. Talk about the age, location and materials used in the different buildings. Include some aerial photographs and a range of settlements from isolated farms to great cities. This is a project which could well extend over a considerable period. **Copymaster 4.18** (Houses World-wide) could be introduced during this activity.

Copymasters

4.15 Street Survey Children should complete this survey when they look at buildings in a street near the school. Explain that they should tick or colour the boxes, working across the rows from the arrow.

4.16 Where I Live This sheet needs to be completed in the classroom with the children discussing each question with the teacher or helper. It illustrates that towns have a much wider range of buildings than villages.

4.17 Houses This copymaster provides a cut-out for a house model. The children will need to colour the cut-out before they glue down the flaps.

4.18 Houses Worldwide Children should colour the pictures of the different houses and discuss which part of the world they might come from. In fact, they come from (top to bottom) Mexico, Indonesia, the United Kingdom and Africa. The children record their answers by ticking the empty boxes.

Homes Around the World

Area of
Study
5

REASONS FOR JOURNEYS

Level 2	>	**Statement of Attainment**

2b) Pupils should be able to give reasons why people make journeys of different lengths.

Example and links with the Programme of Study

The children should ask questions about a particular journey and talk about short and long journeys. Examples could include going shopping, visiting relatives and taking holidays.

Introduction

Movement is an important geographical concept. It includes routes and journeys, different forms of transport, traffic management and the movement of people around the world. This Statement of Attainment focuses on the reasons why people travel. It extends the work on journeys which the children will already have undertaken for this Attainment Target.

There are a number of ideas which children need to grasp in order to meet this Statement of Attainment. For example, they have to realise that the distance between the starting and finishing points of a journey affects the time it takes to complete it. They must also consider the purpose or reason for different journeys.

You could start by talking about the journeys that the children make to school and other places in the locality. You could then consider longer journeys such as coach trips, train travel and holiday destinations. This will introduce a variety of different examples and raise some more general questions about movement patterns.

Key vocabulary

abroad	journey
aeroplane	local
bus	move
car	near
close	obstacles
direction	route
distance	ship
far	train
holiday	travel

Key questions

Why are some journeys longer than others?
What hazards and difficulties get in the way of routes?
How do we know which way to go?
Why do people use different types of transport?
What types of people travel a lot?

Picture books

The Thomas the Tank Engine stories by the Reverend Awdry (published by Kaye & Ward) provide children with a wealth of detail about physical and human geography. The different journeys that the engines make and the routes that they take are ideal source material and could be the basis for class discussions and investigations.

Activity 4.39: Near or far?

Materials needed

Drawing paper, crayons/felt tips, coloured wool, drawing pins, large-scale Ordnance Survey map of the school locality.

Draw a simplified version of the Ordnance Survey map of your school locality and fix it to the wall where all the children can see it. Get each child to identify where they live and mark their home with a drawing pin. The children should then draw pictures of themselves on small pieces of drawing paper. Place each picture next to the correct pin and connect it to the school using wool or string. Finally, overlay three concentric rings to show distance bands – near, medium and far. Discuss the display with the children. Who has the longest and shortest journeys? How long do they take?

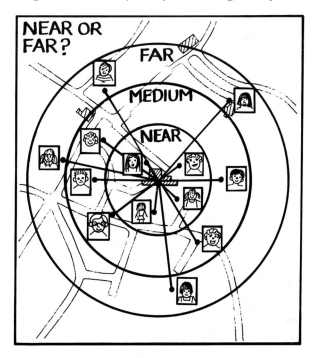

Activity 4.40: Journey to school

Find out more about the children's journey to school. **Copymaster 4.19** (Journey to School) provides a series of structured questions which the children could complete for themselves and take home for parents to check. You could then discuss and compare the results. Do children who live near the school always have the shortest journeys? Which is the longest journey made on foot, and by car? What are the main obstacles and dangers?

Activity 4.41: Journeys around the school

Materials needed
Pins, wool, plan of the school.

Get the children to talk about different journeys they make from the classroom to other parts of the school. They might go to the toilets, other classrooms, the secretary's office, library area, playground, and so on. Using pins and wool, plot these journeys on a large, clear plan of your school. Which are the shortest and longest journeys? Which journeys only involve going through one door? Which journeys involve going through two or three doors? See if the children can make up puzzle journeys which they can describe to each other (the other children have to guess where the journey ends). Use **Copymaster 4.20** (Different Journeys) as a way of developing the work.

Activity 4.42: Reasons for travel

Materials needed
Large, clear plan of the school.

Discuss in detail some of the journeys which the children identified in the previous activity. Use the map as a way of prompting further ideas. What would the children find at the places they have selected? How many different reasons can they think of for going there? What other parts of the school can children visit on their own? What parts do they go to occasionally, and why? Where do they never go?

Activity 4.43: Places to visit

Talk about different sections of the community, such as old age pensioners, teenagers and mothers with young children. What journeys are they likely to make, and for what purpose? What type of transport could they use? Are there any problems which make it hard for them to travel when and where they want to? Explore this idea further using **Copymaster 4.21** (Places to Visit).

Activity 4.44: Journeys for work

Materials needed
Drawing paper, crayons, strips of frieze paper about $\frac{1}{2}$ m long and 15 cm wide, glue.

Think about different people who travel as part of their daily work. Bus drivers, milkmen, postmen/women, police officers and ambulance drivers all move around from place to place for their job. Why do they have to move around? Get the children to make a small frieze showing the journey one of these people makes. They could work in groups, with each child contributing one or two drawings. When the friezes are finished you could either put them up on the wall or mount them in a concertina book so the journey can be seen to unfold.

Activity 4.45: Journey survey

Materials needed
Ordnance Survey map of the local area.

Get the children to keep a record of all the journeys they make over a number of days. **Copymaster 4.22** (Journey Survey) is an empty survey sheet which the children can complete. You should make it clear that they only need to record journeys to specific places. There is no need for them to record every time they go out to play. However, if they go for a walk to the park then that would count. When the survey is complete you should discuss the results. Can the children find the different places on an Ordnance Survey map of the area? What form of transport was used most? What was the main reason for journeys?

Activity 4.46: Holiday journeys

Materials needed
Holiday brochures, large map of the United Kingdom, large map of Europe.

Ask the children if they went away on holiday. Can they bring to school brochures and other details about where they went? What was the name of the nearest town? Was it in the United Kingdom or abroad? What was the country or region? Find the different places on a map and work out the approximate distance. What type of transport did the children use? How did their parents choose the destination?

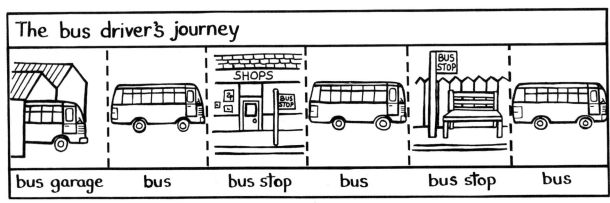

Make a frieze showing where people go in their daily work.

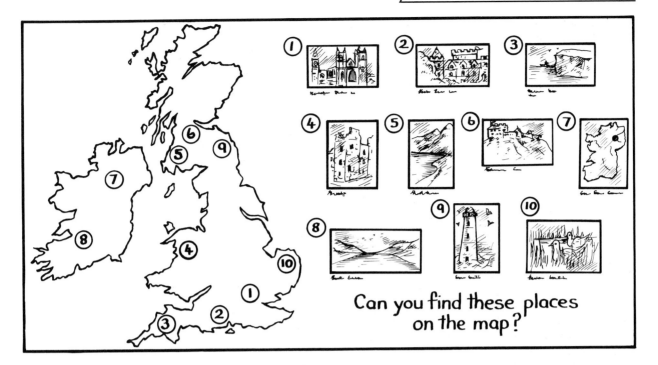

Can you find these places on the map?

Activity 4.47: Postcard corner

Materials needed

Postcards of places the children have visited, map of the United Kingdom.

Set up a display of postcards showing the places both you and the children have visited in the United Kingdom. Write a label under each one saying where it comes from. Include a map in the display. Give each postcard a number. Put the number next to the postcard and at the correct place on the map. You could extend the work by including a wider range of postcards, and talking about the distance to each of the different locations.

Activity 4.48: Adventure journeys

Materials needed

Travel stories, slides and videos, world map or globe.

Read the children some true accounts of journeys of exploration and adventure. These could include safaris, mountain expeditions, long-distance sailing races or space travel. Discuss and map the journeys. Try to find out details of how the people travelled, the dangers that they faced and the things they saw. Why did they go on the journey? Use this information as a stimulus to encourage the children to write some adventure stories of their own. Get them to include some real place names and features from a world map.

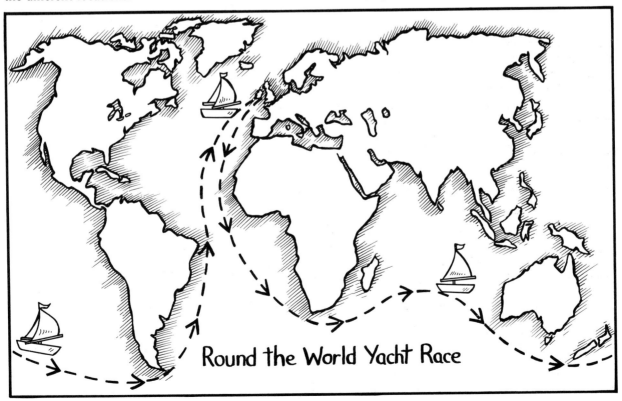

Round the World Yacht Race

Copymasters

4.19 Journey to School   The children should record the details of their journey to school on this copymaster and take it home for their parents to check.

4.20 Different Journeys   This sheet introduces children to the plan of a sample primary school which they then use to record different journeys.

4.21 Places to Visit   This copymaster is designed to illustrate the idea that journeys people make depend on their needs. It is valuable to discuss the places people might visit with the class before children start working individually.

4.22 Journey Survey   Children should use this sheet to record all the journeys that they make to specific places over a period of a couple of days.

 PROVISION OF GOODS AND SERVICES

Area of Study 6

CM 4.23 –4.25

Statement of Attainment

Level 2

2c)   Pupils should be able to identify how goods and services needed in the local community are provided.

Example and links with the Programme of Study
The children should know that food is obtained from local shops, stamps from post offices and newsagents, health care from doctors' surgeries and from hospitals; and that some goods and services are delivered to homes.

Introduction
Modern living depends on an extensive network of distribution systems. Water, electricity, gas and other utilities are brought directly to our homes. Food and other goods are delivered according to demand to hundreds of thousands of shops around the country. Young children need to know not only that farms produce food, but also the process by which it reaches us.

In order to meet this Statement of Attainment, children need to be introduced to the idea of 'goods' and 'services'. There will be plenty of examples in the local environment. You may also be able to draw on the children's experience through conversation and discussion. Once they have understood the basic idea, children can then begin to trace selected goods and services back towards their source or place of origin.

The work could be developed as part of a topic on shops. It also relates to wider themes such as 'Our Town' and 'People Who Help Us'. Where possible, opportunities should be taken to develop map and fieldwork skills.

Key vocabulary

community	food
deliver	gas
distant	goods
electricity	hospital
emergency	local
market	shop
pipe	surgery
post office	telephone
service	water

Key questions
What are goods and services?
What things are provided from local sources?
What things come from distant places?
Which systems depend on pipes and wires?
Which systems depend on transport?
What happens when there is a breakdown?

Picture books
Shopping is a theme that features in quite a number of picture books. *The Shopping Basket* by John Burningham (Cape, 1980) is a humorous tale that involves a whole variety of different animals. *Wilberforce Goes Shopping* by Margaret Gordon (Kestrel, 1983) is one of a series of stories about Wilberforce the bear. Doreen Roberts adopts a more factual approach in *Joe's Day at the Market* (Oxford, 1973).

Song
'My Ship Sailed from China' from *Apusskidu* by Beatrice Harrop (Black, 1975).

Activity 4.49: Goods

Materials needed
Cardboard box, hat, glove, shoe, book, battery, food packets, stone, twig, feather, seashell.

Fill an empty cardboard box with a variety of items. Get the children to sort them into groups. They will probably find various ways of doing this, but after a while you could suggest that they sort them into things which are goods and things which are not. This should then lead to a discussion about where goods come from. **Copymaster 4.23** (Goods) will help to consolidate the children's ideas.

Activity 4.50: Emergency services

Materials needed
Television advertisement for emergency services, *Yellow Pages.*

Show the children a television advertisement which involves emergency services. Most of these are amusing, such as the one featuring a householder who rings for a plumber as his house fills with water. Discuss with the class who is being asked for help, whether they will be paid and what it is they are selling. Look through the *Yellow Pages* to see what other sorts of people offer services and discuss the work that they do. Ask the children to write stories and paint pictures of exciting and amusing emergencies. The stories might capture their imagination and involve a string of incidents (as in the Flanders and Swann song about the gasman). **Copymaster 4.24** (Services) explores this further.

Activity 4.51: Services in school

Materials needed
A large plan of the school.

Investigate services in your school. You could begin by considering the classroom. How are light, heat and water provided? Who organises repairs, cleaning and waste removal? Is any food prepared in the school?

What happens if a child is hurt in the playground? How are messages received and sent? Fix a large plan of the school on to the wall of the classroom. Get the children to add labels for telephones, dustbins, first aid, kitchens, and so on.

Activity 4.52: Role play
Talk with the children about the different people who provide a service, such as doctors, dentists, teachers and police officers. Divide the class into small groups and get them to act out a short scene involving someone who provides a service. Ask them to perform it to the rest of the class. Can the other children work out what is going on? What service is being provided?

Activity 4.53: Race games

Materials needed
Some bags of letters and strips of cloth.

Play some games in PE based on the idea of services. Divide the children into teams and see which team is fastest at 'delivering' the letters. Alternatively, you could give the children some strips of cloth and see which one can bandage up a 'patient' most quickly.

Activity 4.54: Shopping street

Materials needed
Large cardboard boxes, magazines, modelling and artwork materials.

Obtain some large cardboard boxes and cut these in half down the middle. Working in small groups or individually, the children can then use the boxes to

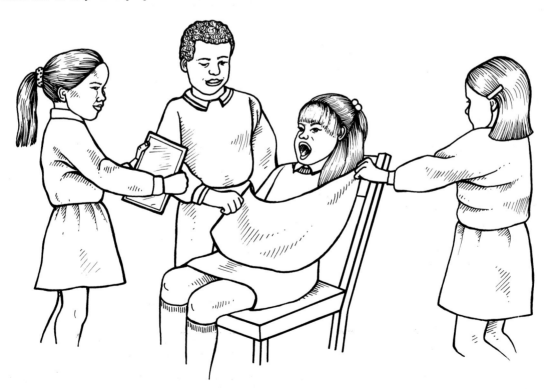

Roleplay. Ask the children to act out a scene.

The newsagent   The grocer's   The chemist

Shopping street. Make models of shops from cardboard boxes.

make some model shops. They will need to decide what their shop sells. Is it a chemist, newsagent or grocer's? Get the children to give their shop a name, and see if they can find any pictures of goods in magazines to cut out and put on the 'shelves'. When they are finished you could arrange the models along one of the walls of the classroom to make a shopping street. If the children put flaps across the shop windows you might get other children to guess what each shop sells.

Activity 4.55: Adopt a shop
Either working as a class or in groups, 'adopt' one of the shops in the neighbourhood. Ask the shopkeeper to come and talk about what he or she does. When does the shop open and close? Who works there? When do they go on holiday? Where do the goods come from? How long has the shop been there? See if the shopkeeper can explain about ordering stock. How do the people running the shop decide what to order? How is it done, and who delivers the goods?

Activity 4.56: Markets
Materials needed
Plasticine, photographs of markets around the world.

Make a plasticine model of a market stall. It might be selling food, clothes, household goods or electrical equipment. Put different models together to make a complete scene. The children might then add live-stock. They could record the layout on a plan. Talk to the children about markets they have visited. Why do people still like to use them when big stores sell goods in more comfortable surroundings? Widen the discussion by looking at photographs of markets around the world. What can you learn from the pictures? What are the similarities and differences from markets in the United Kingdom?

Activity 4.57: Networks
Materials needed
Large pieces of paper, crayons.

Organise a short walk round the streets near your school. Get the children to look for all the different goods and services clues they can find. These might include telephone boxes, fire hydrants, manhole covers in the pavement, shop signs, and so on. Use **Copymaster 4.25** (Different Clues) as a way of recording information. What can the children learn from the things they have discovered? Can they describe other parts of the network and see how they link together? Make rubbings of a variety of manhole and other pavement covers. Put them up as a class display and arrange them in groups – water, gas, electricity and telephone.

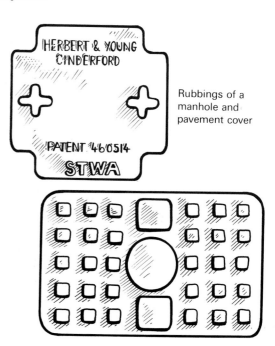

Rubbings of a manhole and pavement cover

108

Activity 4.58: Local goods and services

Materials needed

Map of the local area, card for labels.

Talk with the children about the different goods and services which are produced in your area. A country area will have farms, on the coast there could be fishing, along rivers gravel works are quite common, towns have industrial buildings and factories. Do the children know the location of the nearest power station, reservoir, main post office, milk depot, and so on? Make some labels and pin them on to a map at the correct point.

Activity 4.59: Goods and services overseas

Materials needed

Resource packs, slides and films about an overseas country.

Look at some pictures, slides or films of daily life in a country overseas. It might be best to choose a country in the tropics where conditions are significantly different from those in the United Kingdom. Ask the children about the things they notice. How are goods and services provided? What surprises the children most? What similarities and differences do they notice?

Copymasters

4.23 Goods This copymaster is designed to reinforce the idea that goods are things which people have worked to produce, and that they are therefore sold for money.

4.24 Services The children should complete the sentences on the sheet to illustrate the range of different services that they use.

4.25 Different Clues This is a recording sheet for use in local streets and buildings. The children should tick the empty boxes when they find each item.

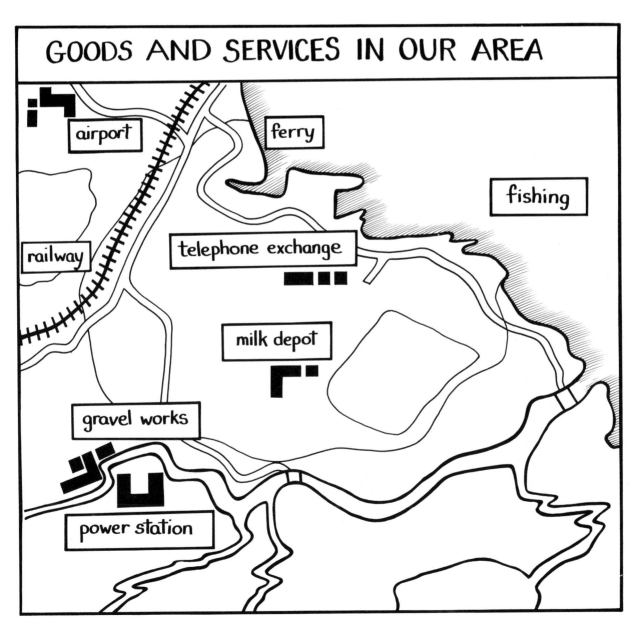

GOODS AND SERVICES IN OUR AREA

WORKING TOWARDS LEVEL 3 ▶

Programme of Study	School-based work	Contrasting area study	World dimension
Pupils should be taught how land is used in different ways . . . and why different amounts of land are required for different purposes.	How are different spaces used in your school? Which activity takes the most space – movement, learning or administration? Can you devise a map to show these differences?	What different types of land use can you identify – parks, factories, shopping centres, and so on? How much space do they take up? Why do they need this amount of space?	Where would you find a prairie farm, skiing resort, safari park or international airport? What special types of land do they need?
Pupils should be taught why different means of transport may be used for different purposes, and how people and goods transfer from one means of transport to another.	How are things sent from class to class? How are goods moved around the school? Which routes/places are the busiest?	What public transport services are found in the area? How are emergency services provided? Are there any through routes?	What different types of transport are used around the world – ships, planes, railways, animals, and so on? What are the advantages and disadvantages of each method?
Pupils should be taught why people move homes.	Are any classes or rooms in your school too crowded? Can you devise a poster encouraging other children to come to your school?	How many children in the class have moved home? Have any of them come from another area? Why did they move?	What different groups of people move around the world? What causes people to become refugees? How can we help refugees?
Pupils should be taught how the functions and origins of settlements may be revealed by their current features.	Is there any evidence of change in your school? Are there any empty classrooms, mobile classrooms, new rooms?	What are the new buildings in the area? Are there any very old ones? What were they used for?	What are the main routes in different parts of the world? What are the cities which have grown up along them?

ATTAINMENT TARGET 5: ENVIRONMENTAL GEOGRAPHY

Pupils should demonstrate their increasing knowledge and understanding of:

i)   the use and misuse of natural resources;
ii) the quality and vulnerability of different environments; and
iii) the possibilities for protecting and managing environments.

Programme of Study for Key Stage 1 (Levels 1 & 2 only. For Level 3 see p. 131)

Environmental geography

Pupils should be taught:

- where common materials are obtained, *for example, wool from sheep, rock from quarries, fish from the sea*, and how they are extracted;
- to discuss and explain their likes and dislikes about features of their environment, for example, *'What is good about where we live?', 'What spoils it?'*;
- to identify activities which have changed the environment and to consider ways in which they can improve their own environment.

ABOUT THIS ATTAINMENT TARGET

In recent years, environmental issues have figured more and more prominently in the geography curriculum. This reflects a growing concern about what is happening to our surroundings and the changes that are beginning to occur on a continental and global scale. The Working Group which devised the National Curriculum decided to highlight the environment by allocating it a separate Attainment Target. It was a decision which was particularly welcomed by the Secretary of State for Education at the time.

Young children are often surprisingly knowledgeable about environmental issues. They receive information about current environmental initiatives from the television, radio and other media sources. Some children may have direct experience of participating in a simple recycling project or helping in a conservation scheme. By the time they come to school quite a few children have gathered a wide variety of information on the environment.

There are plenty of opportunities for introducing and examining environmental themes. On a personal level, you can encourage children to use resources wisely and conserve scarce energy. Teachers have always sought to stop children being wasteful.

On a more general level, you can study the school and the immediate neighbourhood to look for examples of pollution. You could extend the work by making contacts with local community groups. It is important to consider ways of solving environmental problems so that children are not left with the negative impression that there is nothing they can do. Our individual actions can, collectively, have an enormous impact. This is demonstrated by the phenomenal growth of 'green consumerism'. In addition, specific pressure groups, such as Friends of the Earth and Greenpeace, have shown what can be achieved through determined action.

111

BACKGROUND INFORMATION FOR THE TEACHER ▶

Facts and figures

- Half the rubbish we throw away could be recycled.

- A car produces approximately four times its own weight of carbon dioxide a year.

- World population is increasing by over a million people each week.

- Half of the world's plants and animals could become extinct in the next sixty years.

- By the middle of the next century world temperatures are expected to rise by between 1.5 and 4.5°C.

The environmental crisis is a relatively new phenomenon. It has been prompted partly by the development of industry and technology, and partly by the sheer growth of the human population. In the last 40 years manufacturing industry has increased sevenfold and world population has approximately doubled. This has put the environment under more and more stress.

Natural resources
The problem is compounded by the unequal distribution of resources. The world's richest nations, North America, Europe, Japan and Australasia, possess nearly all the world's wealth and are responsible for creating most of the pollution. By contrast, many people in Africa, southern Asia and Latin America live in great poverty and are forced to exploit the environment in order to survive.

Vulnerable environments
Many experts agree that the next decade will be critical as far as the environment is concerned. Acid rain, nuclear radiation, desertification and the clearance of the rainforests are some of the issues which are hitting the headlines on an almost daily basis. The most serious threat of all is perhaps the prospect of irreversible climate change caused by greenhouse gases. It is, however, in the nature of environmental problems that they are all interrelated.

Managing the environment
There are many different things we can do to tackle the problems. Greater social justice, more efficient use of resources, recycling and sustainable development all offer encouraging possibilities. Children and adults alike need to be well informed so that they can make sensible choices. There can be little doubt that this Attainment Target addresses one of the central issues of our times.

NAME MATERIALS

CM 5.1
–5.7

Level	**Statement of Attainment**
1	1a) Pupils should be able to identify and name materials obtained from natural resources.

Example and links with the Programme of Study

Children should investigate common materials in their own surroundings. They should study a range of products such as food, wood and coal, and find out where they come from and how they are obtained.

Introduction

We depend on natural resources in many different ways. Our homes are built from stone, wood and clay, our clothes are derived from plants and animals, our food is the product of the soil. Many young children will be unaware of these links, and you should be careful not to take anything for granted.

You could introduce this Statement of Attainment by talking about the physical surroundings. These will include woods and countryside, farms and mines, and different plants and animals. The children can then explore goods and materials that come from these different places. Much fun can be had spotting and identifying things in the classroom, school and home environment. There is also scope for exhibitions and displays which children can touch and handle.

Key vocabulary

animal	materials
brick	mine
coal	oil
country	quarry
cow	rock
factory	sea
farm	sheep
fish	stone
food	vegetables
forest	wood

Key questions

What things in the classroom have been made by people?
What things in the classroom have not been made by people?
Which things come from plants?
Which things come from animals?
Which things come from underground?

Picture books

If you want to focus on building materials you could read the children the story of 'The Three Little Pigs'. The first one made his home from straw, the second from wood and the third from stone. Alternatively, you might consider food. This is one of the themes in The

Tale of Peter Rabbit by Beatrix Potter. The adventure begins when Peter Rabbit squeezes under the gate into Mr McGregor's garden.

Rhyme

If all the World were Paper

If all the world were paper,
And all the sea were ink,
And all the trees were bread and cheese,
What should we do for drink?

Activity 5.1: Natural resources

Materials needed

A collection of natural resources, cardboard labels.

Make a collection of a variety of natural resources such as wood, stone, coal, sand, wool, cotton, leather, clay and oil. You could either provide all of these yourself or get the children to bring in items of their own from home. Write out a label for each one, talk about their origins and discuss why they are 'natural' resources. Get the children to put the labels in the right place. Take the labels away each morning before school and see if the children can replace them correctly.

Activity 5.2: Associations

Materials needed

Class display of natural resources (see Activity 5.1), a selection of objects made from these resources.

Help the children to understand how natural resources are turned into things we need. Add a selection of objects to the class display (see Activity 5.1). For example, you might include a glove or a piece of carpet. Can the children associate them with the wool? Add other items, such as plastic and cellophane. Try to mix obvious and not-so-obvious objects and play a daily matching game linking resources with products.

Activity 5.3: Resources in the classroom

Do a survey of objects in the classroom. Discuss the natural resources that are used in each thing. Pin or stick the labels from the class display (see Activity 5.1) on to the items with which they are associated. For example, the label saying wood should be fixed to the table, sand to the glass and clay to the bricks.

Activity 5.4: Resources and products mobile

Materials needed
Scissors, crayons, string, glue, cardboard.

Get the children to draw a picture of one type of natural resource and a picture of something that has been obtained from it. Examples might include milk from cows, metal from rocks and books from trees. Make a mobile by arranging the drawings in pairs. Put the resource at the top and the product underneath. You could use **Copymaster 5.1** (What is it made of?) as a way of introducing the activity, or to help children who find it hard to think of examples to draw. You could extend the work by asking the children to make a mobile of all the things they can think of that are made of wood, wool or oil. Not only does this make an attractive classroom display, it also helps to highlight the properties of different natural resources.

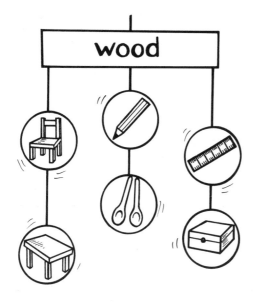

Activity 5.5: Wood rubbings

Materials needed
Large wax crayons, greaseproof paper.

Make a series of rubbings of wooden objects around your class and school. You could mount these as a display with labels saying what they show. If possible, take a photograph of each object and put it next to the appropriate rubbings. This will help to set them in context. Discuss the rubbings with the children and get them to suggest suitable descriptive words, such as rough, smooth, swirling, straight. Extend the work using **Copymaster 5.2** (Trees are Wood).

Activity 5.6: Woollen clothes

Materials needed
Collection of woollen clothes, different types of wool.

Look at your collection of woollen clothing. Decide how it is possible to tell if the material is wool. The children might feel its texture, look at it carefully, check the label, look for the 'pure new wool' logo, and so on. Arrange for a weaver or knitter to come and talk to the children about what they do. If possible, contact a local farm and arrange for the children to see a sheep. This will introduce them to the 'resource' in a very practical and direct manner.

Activity 5.7: Miniature characters

Materials needed
Wool, rings of cardboard, buttons, glue.

Do some simple weaving with scraps of wool, or make a woollen ball which can be turned into a miniature character.

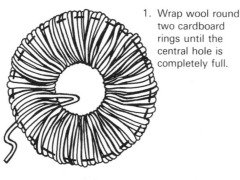

1. Wrap wool round two cardboard rings until the central hole is completely full.

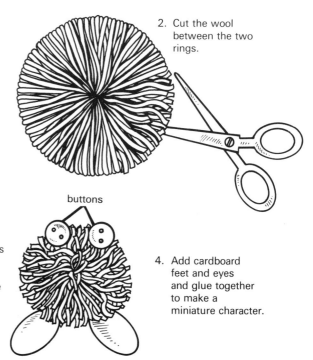

2. Cut the wool between the two rings.

3. Insert a separate strand of wool between the rings and tie the woollen ball securely. Remove the rings.

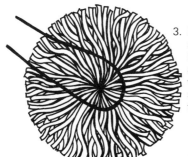

buttons

4. Add cardboard feet and eyes and glue together to make a miniature character.

How to make miniature characters

114

CLOTHES SHOP

Set up a market stall for the goods which the children have made. Design a package, cost the materials and find out a 'commercial price' for the products. Make an advertisement to encourage people to buy them.

Activity 5.8: Clothes shop

Materials needed
Photographs of clothing from magazines.

Ask the children to cut out photographs of clothing from magazines. Arrange the pictures as a collage on a display board. See if you can make it look like a clothes shop. Add labels for each item of clothing saying what it is and the material which it is made from.

Activity 5.9: Made of iron and steel

Materials needed
Magnets.

Go for a walk round your school to find materials made of iron. Give the children magnets so that they can carry out simple tests. They can record their results using **Copymaster 5.5** (Made of Iron and Steel). They could also take rubbings of any iron objects which have interesting patterns. When you return to the classroom make a list of all the objects the children have discovered and add this to a class display.

Activity 5.10: Zig-zag book

Materials needed
Reference books on iron and steel-making, hammers, nails, card, glue.

Make a storybook about the life of a nail. You will need reference books to find out how iron ore is dug out of the ground and made into steel in a furnace. Mount a number of different nails in the book. Write down how they are used. For example, small pins are used in picture frames while large masonry nails secure window and door frames. Find some hammers to go in a display with the book.

Activity 5.11: Paper making

Materials needed

Scraps of tissue paper, kitchen roll and newspaper.

Make some sheets of paper from scraps of tissue paper, kitchen roll and newspaper. Pulp the pieces together in water and spread the sheets out on a frame to dry. Find out from reference books where pulp comes from.

Activity 5.12: Butter making

Materials needed

Cream from the top of milk, plastic bottles, refrigerator, salt, biscuits.

Collect the cream from the top of some bottles of milk. Pour it into some empty plastic bottles and get the children to shake them until the cream thickens to butter. Add a little salt and put the butter in a refrigerator until it hardens. Spread the finished product on biscuits to see what it tastes like. Discuss the ways butter is used in home cooking.

Activity 5.13: Food from different places

Materials needed

Food labels, wool or cotton, world map.

Make a collection of labels from packets and tins. Look at them in turn and find out which foods come from the United Kingdom and which ones from other countries. Arrange the labels in a display around a map of the world. Fix lines of wool or cotton linking the labels to the correct countries.

Activity 5.14: Animal, vegetable or mineral?

Give the children a questionnaire to find out about the different ways natural resources are used in their homes. **Copymaster 5.7** (Animal, Vegetable or Mineral?) provides a format which you could use. Alternatively, the children could devise questions of their own.

Discuss the results when the children return to school. What natural resources are used most? Is there any reason for this?

Copymasters

5.1 What is it made of? Children can colour this sheet and cut out the drawings to make a mobile. The sheep (the resource) should come at the top of the mobile, with the jumper (the product) underneath.

5.2 Trees are Wood The aim of this sheet is to illustrate the fact that wooden things come from trees. Children should use the space inside the tree to draw a wooden item of their choice. They can then colour the tree as a kind of frame.

5.3 Made of Wood (1) In this survey children explore the classroom to see if they can find the things shown in the drawings. They should colour or tick the empty boxes for each one they discover.

5.4 Made of Wood (2) This second survey resembles the previous one, except that it should be conducted at home with the children working on their own.

5.5 Made of Iron and Steel Children could use this sheet in a variety of ways. They could draw just one item made of iron, choose three or four of the most interesting items they have discovered, or list all the things in their survey.

5.6 Material Puzzle The aim of this activity is to reinforce the link between resources and products. Children should begin by colouring the pictures and cutting them out. They should then see if they can put them together again in the correct order.

5.7 Animal, Vegetable or Mineral? Children can use this survey sheet to collect information about the objects in their home. At the simplest level they could put a tick in the correct box for each thing they discover. More able children could name the things or make small drawings of them. It may also be possible to enlist the parents' help and get them to write down what the children find out.

 PERSONAL LIKES AND DISLIKES

CM 5.8 –5.12

Area of Study 2

Level 2

Statement of Attainment

1 b) Pupils should be able to express personal likes and dislikes about features of the local area.

Example and links with the Programme of Study

The children should be encouraged to formulate very simple judgements about the local area. They might discuss the things which they think are 'good' and the things which they think are 'bad'. This will involve using words such as 'noisy', 'quiet', 'dull', 'interesting', 'smelly', 'smoky', 'ugly' and 'beautiful'.

Introduction

The quality of the environment is fundamental to our standard of living. People are becoming increasingly aware of the threats to the natural world, and are seeking ways to protect it for the future. This Statement of Attainment focuses on the child's subjective response and asks them to consider what they like and dislike in their surroundings.

The statement is deceptively simple. Ideally, children should be encouraged to give reasons for their opinions, not to make snap judgements. They should also appreciate that other people think differently about the same things. These are heavy demands for infants.

One of the best approaches is to develop basic descriptive vocabulary. Children can be encouraged to consider the physical environment by talking about rivers, hills, parks, and other landscape features. They could look at what people do to the environment and consider what facilities are lacking in their own neighbourhood. If they are given a chance to work in groups, this will help them to develop a balanced viewpoint. Whatever approach you adopt, remember to respect individual sensibilities if the streets and homes where children live are considered in any of the work that you organise.

Key vocabulary

beautiful	noisy
buildings	park
church	people
damage	place
dislike	quiet
dull	rubbish
factory	smelly
house	smoky
interesting	spoil
like	ugly

Key questions

What do you like and dislike about your school? Why?
Are the things you like always good?
Are the things you dislike always bad?
What can you do about the things you dislike?

Folk tales

'The Fisherman and his Wife' by the Brothers Grimm is a powerful story of greed which raises questions about how we respond to our surroundings. You could use it as a way of getting the children to talk about what they like and dislike.

Picture books

The contrast between urban and rural environments is explored in the well-known story of the town mouse and the country mouse. There are a number of picture-book versions including *The Town Mouse and the Country Mouse* by Paul Galdone (Bodley, 1971). *The Tale of Johnny Town Mouse* by Beatrix Potter considers the same theme in a different way and concludes 'one place suits one person, another place suits another person'. Another delightful picture book is Brian Wildsmith's *Daisy* (Oxford, 1984). This tells the story of Daisy the cow who escapes from her field and goes to see the world, but decides that her own field is best after all.

Activity 5.15: Things we like in school

Get the children to make a list of all the things they like about their class and school. Ask them to make drawings of some of their favourite things. Mount the drawings in a class book with sentences under each one explaining what is good about it.

Activity 5.16: Sensory walk

Plan a sensory walk around the school. What unpleasant sounds and smells do the children notice? What things do they like the feel of? You could use **Copymaster 5.8** (Smells I Don't Like), **Copymaster 5.9** (Sounds I Don't Like) and **Copymaster 5.10** (Things I Like to Touch) to record the information. Alternatively, you could get the children to express their opinions by voting for individual items. For example, how many children like the smell of polish in the hall? How many dislike it? The information from the survey can be displayed as a simple block graph. Unifix blocks are ideal for this purpose and can lead to further work on a computer.

POLISH SMELL

like   dislike

6 children liked the smell of polish in the hall.
3 children disliked it.

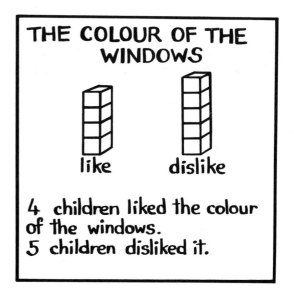

THE COLOUR OF THE WINDOWS

like   dislike

4 children liked the colour of the windows.
5 children disliked it.

Word game. The children pin their words to different items.

Activity 5.17: Word game

Materials needed
Set of flash cards, Blu-Tack.

Make a set of flash cards using the words from **Copymaster 5.11** (Word Game). Teach the children how to read the words using the flash card technique. Then give each child the copymaster sheet and ask them to make their own set of word cards. Play the Word Game, getting the children to express their likes and dislike of eight items in the class or school by fixing the cards to them using Blu-Tack. You will need to agree with the children what items they are going to select, and explain that the cards must be placed face down so that the word is not visible. The children are allowed to put their cards in the same place as each other's, as long as they do not overlap.

When all the cards have been used up, you should turn them over while the children watch. Do all the cards say the same thing? Make a list of the objects selected, and record if they are mostly liked, mostly disliked, or both liked and disliked.

Activity 5.18: The local environment
Go for a sensory walk in the local environment. What smells, sounds, sights and surfaces do the children like and dislike? Use **Copymaster 5.12** (Different Places) to

record this information. Could anything be done to improve the places which are generally disliked? How would the children introduce more of the things that they like? Choose some of the best ideas, get the children to illustrate them, and send their suggestions off to the local council Planning Department.

Activity 5.19: Different features
Make a list of all the features which the children generally think make something likeable. You might consider colour, shape, texture, perfume, natural sounds, and so on. Using this list, test the school and locality to see how these features are used. Are there any obvious gaps or omissions? How do the children think the environment might be improved?

Activity 5.20: Different opinions

Materials needed
Outline plan of the school.

Ask the children to design two different signs. One should say 'I like this place', the other should say 'I dislike this place'. Place the signs on your plan of the school.

Ask other people what they think. You might invite the headteacher, the caretaker, a parent or visitor to

118

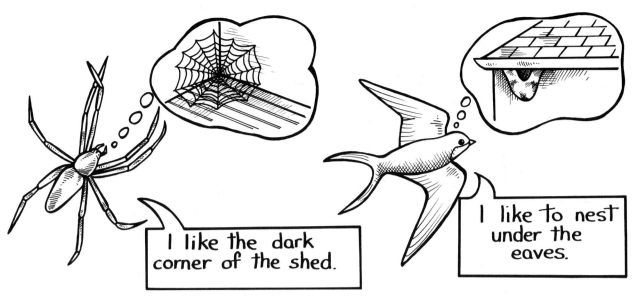

Different opinions. What makes an ideal environment?

give their views. Record the different opinions on a table or chart.

Consider the places a bird, mouse, spider and other creatures would like in and around your school. What are the things they would want in their ideal environment? Draw pictures of different creatures with dream bubbles showing their favourite place. Add a sentence underneath describing what each picture shows.

Activity 5.21: Likes and dislikes

Materials needed

Artwork materials.

Ask the children to paint a picture or draw a map of their journey to school. Discuss the things they like on the route. Do they pass any places they dislike? Make a list using a table with two columns with the headings

'likes' and 'dislikes'. Make a display of the pictures and maps and add the lists underneath.

Activity 5.22: Good for children

Materials needed

Artwork materials, map of your local area.

Talk about places in the locality which are good for children. Which places are dangerous? Get the children to do drawings of as many places, safe and unsafe, as they can think of. If they think the place is dangerous they should put a red circle round the drawing. If they think it is safe they should put a blue rectangle round the edge. Arrange the drawings around a map of the locality and add the heading 'Safe and Dangerous Places'.

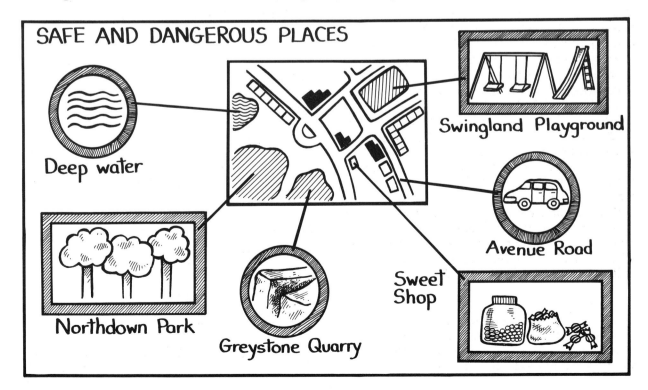

Activity 5.23: A far-away place

Materials needed

Postcards, pictures and photographs of a distant place.

Get the children to look at postcards and pictures of a place beyond their locality. Discuss what they like and dislike about each one. You might have a checklist of questions covering the physical features, buildings and settlements, and the quality of the environment. If possible, arrange for someone who has been to this place to come and talk to the children. Are they able to confirm or deny what the children have deduced from the pictures? What did they like and dislike about the place?

Copymasters

5.8 Smells I Don't Like   Use this copymaster to record information on a sensory walk around the school or local environment. Children can either write or draw in the empty boxes. Helpers and assistants could also make notes to help children who may not be able to put their thoughts on paper.

5.9 Sounds I Don't Like   This copymaster is also intended to record children's opinions and reactions on a sensory walk.

5.10 Things I Like to Touch   This is the final copymaster in a set of three for use on sensory walks in the school or out of doors.

5.11 Word Game   Children should cut up the words on this sheet and fix them to appropriate objects and items around the school as part of a game (see Activity 5.17).

5.12 Different Places   This recording sheet could be used either in school or in the local area to encourage children to think more deeply about the character of different places.

Area of Study 3

OBTAINING NATURAL MATERIALS

CM 5.13 –5.16

Statement of Attainment

Level 2

2a)   Pupils should be able to identify how people obtain materials from the environment.

Example and links with the Programme of Study

Children should be taught how materials are obtained through quarrying, mining, fishing and lumbering.

Introduction

Industry can be divided into three main categories. Primary industries obtain raw materials from the natural environment, secondary industries turn these materials into goods we can use, while tertiary industries provide goods and services. This Statement of Attainment directs attention to primary industries. Quarrying, mining, forestry and fishing are key examples which have featured on the geography curriculum for many years.

You could introduce the work by considering primary industry in your own locality. Are there any mines or quarries near your school? If not, why not? Where is the nearest forestry plantation or fishing port? Have any children been there? You could then consider the processes by which materials are obtained. Children might investigate how a quarry works and how fish are caught. In addition, they should find out how different raw materials are brought to the place where they live. The coal merchant, fish shop and timber yard are the outlets at the end of a chain that leads back to an industrial source.

Many primary industries are isolated in rural locations, and public access is limited due to the dangers of the sites. Some, such as mining and fishing, have also declined dramatically in recent years. As a result, few children will have direct experience of the processes involved. It will be important to associate everyday objects with the raw materials from which they are made. If it is possible to arrange a visit to a local site this will obviously make a big impression.

Key vocabulary

coal	port
colliery	quarry
fish	rock
forest	stone
harbour	trawler
lorry	trees
mine	wood
oil	

Key questions

Where do different materials come from?
What comes from underground?
How do we use trees?
How are different goods produced?
How do they reach us?

Rhymes

One, Two, Three, Four, Five

One, two, three, four, five,
Once I caught a fish alive.
Six, seven, eight, nine, ten,
Then I let it go again.

Why did you let it go?
Because it bit my finger so.
Which finger did it bite?
This little finger on the right.

Baa, Baa, Black Sheep

Baa, baa, black sheep,
Have you any wool?
Yes, sir, yes, sir,
Three bags full:
One for the master,
And one for the dame,
And one for the little boy
Who lives down the lane.

Activity 5.24: Raw materials

Materials needed
Map of your locality.

Make a list of any materials which are obtained from your area. Get the children to talk about the things they see or notice. For example, 'We see big lorries carrying chalk through the village', 'We hear the saws in the forest' or 'The railway trucks with cement go past my house'. Are the children able to name any of the places where these things come from? You might find it helpful to have a map of the local area available so that they can point out the different sites.

Activity 5.25: Farming, fishing and mining

Talk about the people who earn their living obtaining materials from the environment. Examples include quarry workers, fishermen, farmers, miners and lumberjacks. Do the children know anybody who has one of these jobs? If possible, arrange for them to come and talk to the class, and get them to bring some tools and specialist equipment with them. Alternatively, you might be able to set up a small exhibition of people at work using posters and photographs. Some local museums have equipment which they are able to loan to schools on request.

Activity 5.26: Machines

Materials needed
Toy machines, models, plans of a port, quarry and farm.

Make a collection of models and toys that might be used in a port, quarry and farm. You will need tractors, combine harvesters, fishing boats, diggers, and so on.

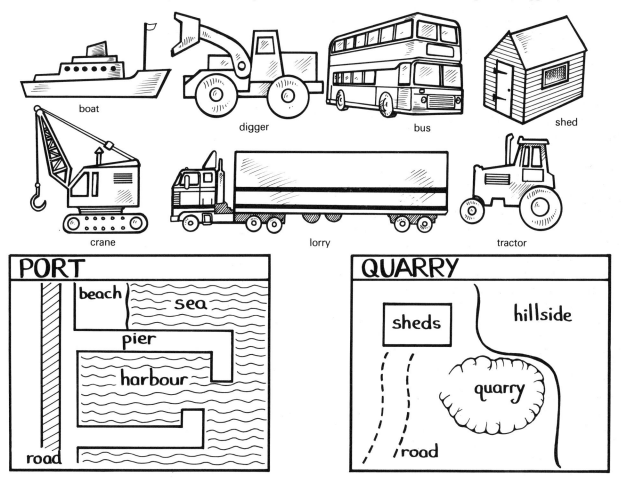

Machines. Get the children to place their toys on plans of different sites.

Get the children to group the toys into mini-scenes. When they are familiar with the toys you could extend the work by providing simple plans for the different sites. Keep the plans and toys in a box so that the children have to sort them into groups each time they use them. Check that they understand where the machines belong on the plans and encourage them to experiment with different arrangements. **Copymaster 5.13** (Machines) is designed to help children understand more about the machines and equipment used in extractive industries, and relates closely to this activity.

Activity 5.27: Different sources

Materials needed
Basic materials and equipment for artwork.

Make a survey of the classroom or school. Decide which items come from under the ground, which ones come from farms, which ones come from trees and which ones come from the sea. Get the children to draw pictures of different things in their survey and put them up as a wall display under these four different headings.

Activity 5.28: Quarry trail
Organise a quarry trail around the school. Get the children to look for things made from stone, iron, sand, clay, chalk and gravel. Children can record their

findings using **Copymaster 5.14** (Quarry Trail). When they have finished the trail, the children should compare their results to see what different things they have discovered. Which materials seem most common? What reasons can they give for this?

Activity 5.29: How are they obtained?
Discuss the different ways materials are obtained from the natural environment. Clay is *dug* out of the ground, stone is *cut* in quarries, coal is *mined* under the ground, crops are *harvested* on farms. Make a collection of the different words that describe these activities. Get the children to complete **Copymaster 5.15** (Different Methods) and play a game of snap using the words and picture cards.

Activity 5.30: Deliveries

Materials needed
Yellow Pages directory, map of the local area, card and other modelling equipment.

Look in the local *Yellow Pages* to find the nearest suppliers for coal, fish, cement and stone. Make up a wall map with copies or cut-outs of the different advertisements. Use the map to work out the route that different delivery vehicles would take to your school. Get the children to make a vehicle to deliver a bag of coal or a block of stone, using card and other modelling materials.

Different sources. Make a survey of everyday items.

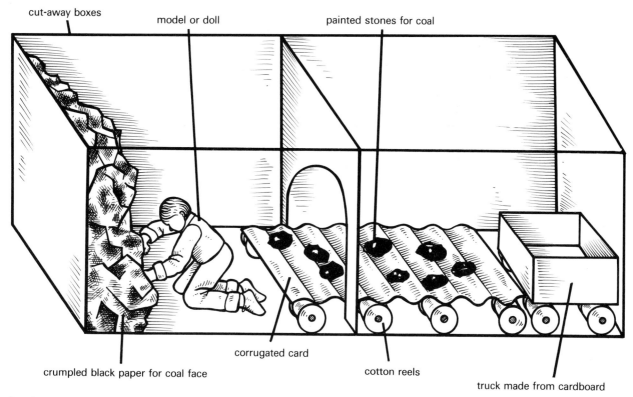

cut-away boxes   model or doll   painted stones for coal

corrugated card

crumpled black paper for coal face   cotton reels

truck made from cardboard

Coal mine model

Activity 5.31: Underground scene

Materials needed

Posters and pictures of mines, old shoe boxes, black paper, corrugated card, cotton reels, cardboard, small dolls, fabric.

Find a poster or some photographs of a coal mine that you can use in a class display. Use this as the reference source for making a model of an underground scene. The children could join a couple of old shoe boxes together to make a tunnel, and fill one end with black paper to represent the coal face. Corrugated card is a simple way of giving the impression of a conveyor belt, and the coal can be made from painted pebbles. Complete the scene by adding a figure or two digging out the coal, and make a few simple trucks from cardboard to place at the other end.

Activity 5.32: Fishing fleet

Materials needed

Margarine tubs, cardboard, Sellotape, paint, pictures and photographs of fishing boats, netting.

Get the children to make some model fishing boats. They could use a margarine tub for the hull and make the bridge from cardboard and Sellotape. When they have finished, ask the children to paint their boats and give them each a name. Put the models on a cardboard base to make a fishing fleet and build harbour walls round the edge.

Collect postcards and photographs of fishing boats and add them to the display. Pin some netting to one of the corners and ask the children to paint and cut out some drawings of fish. Discuss what happens to fish when they are caught.

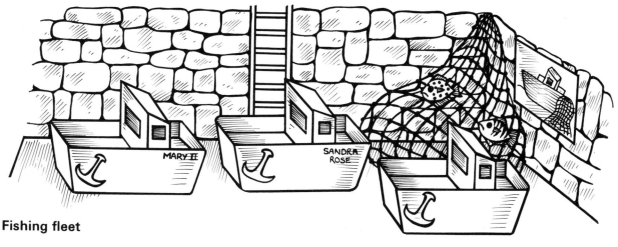

Fishing fleet

Activity 5.33: Fish mobile

Materials needed

Cardboard, hoop, light string, glue.

Make a mobile of fish in the sea with a trawler and net. Begin by asking the children to colour and cut out the fish in **Copymaster 5.16** (Fish). Glue the fish on to a strip of card as a frieze and cut the top in an undulating pattern to represent waves. Fix the card round a hoop and suspend the mobile from the ceiling using light string. Complete the display by adding a drawing of a trawler and a net.

Copymasters

5.13 Machines Get the children to colour the lines from the machines to the materials with which they are associated. To avoid confusion, the children should use a different colour for each line.

5.14 Quarry Trail Use this copymaster to record different materials around your school which have come from a quarry. The children could either name or draw the items they discover in the different data files.

5.15 Different Methods Ask the children to colour the drawings and cut out the cards on this sheet. They can then play a game of snap with a partner, matching the pictures to the correct word. If possible, reproduce the sheet on light card to make the snap cards more durable.

5.16 Fish This copymaster provides children with an outline fish which they can colour and add to a fish frieze or mobile.

Fish mobile

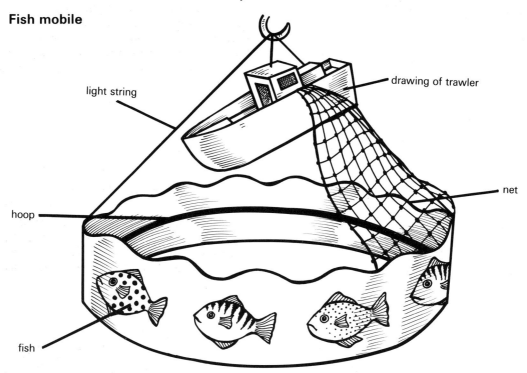

 CHANGING THE ENVIRONMENT

Area of Study 4

CM 5.17 –5.20

Statement of Attainment

Level 2

2b) Pupils should be able to describe ways in which people have changed the environment.

Example and links with the Programme of Study
Children should be taught how people have cultivated the land for farming, built houses and roads, set aside land for leisure, and polluted water.

Introduction

Human activity has had an enormous impact on the environment. For centuries people have struggled to eke out a living from the land, and competed against the elements for survival. Modern technology has changed all this. We now have unprecedented power to alter the world for our own ends. With this power comes new responsibilities.

Children tend to believe that the world into which they have been born has always been the same. They need to be introduced to the idea that at one time in the past all places were countryside. It is hard even for adults to imagine that large cities and towns are a relatively recent phenomenon. Young children can only be expected to develop a piecemeal understanding of how people have changed their surroundings.

One of the best ways of introducing this Statement of Attainment is to consider the changes which have affected the children in their own lifetime. Examples might include moving house, changes in the garden, the acquisition of pets, a new baby in the family, and so on. The children could then discuss small-scale changes to their environment. You could group these into different categories, such as new roads and buildings, changes in the countryside, pollution and conservation. Depending on the age and ability of the children, you might decide to extend the discussion to cover a greater timescale and thereby enlarge their understanding of environmental change.

Key vocabulary

buildings	nature
change	park
country	people
environment	pollution
farm	road
fumes	surroundings
litter	world

Key questions

How old is it?
What was there before?
How have my home and school changed?
Who causes these changes?
What changes happen very slowly?
What changes happen very quickly?

Picture books

In the last few years there has been a spate of exc… picture books on pollution and environmental the These include: *Oi! Get off our Train* by John Burn…ig-ham (Cape, 1989), *The World that Jack built* by Ruth Brown (Andersen, 1990), *Rainforest* by Helen Coucher (Deutsch, 1988), *One World* by Michael Foreman (Andersen, 1990).

Songs

'Air', 'Leave Them a Flower' and 'Across the Hills' are some of the songs about pollution in *The Jolly Herring* by Roger Bush (A & C Black, 1980).

Activity 5.34: Things which change

Working as a class, make a list of different things which change. Examples might include the weather, day and night, plants, animals and people. Display the list and get the children to make drawings of some of the things they have mentioned. **Copymaster 5.17** (Things which Change) will help to develop this activity.

Activity 5.35: Change dial

Materials needed

Circles of card, scissors, glue, split pins.

Using **Copymaster 5.18** (Change Dial), get the children to make a series of 'before' and 'after' pictures of something that changes. They should then mount their pictures on a circular piece of card. Cut a window or opening in a second piece of card large enough to reveal just one of the pictures at a time. Assemble the

split pin

baby girl granny mother

CHANGE

Drawing of change mounted on card

Card circle with 'window'

Change dial

125

two pieces with a split pin in the centre and ask the children to write the word 'change' on the front.

Activity 5.36: Farms and factories

Materials needed

Toy vehicles, animals and buildings, posters and pictures of farms and factories.

Collect posters and pictures which show farm and factory scenes. Ask the children to bring in toys which relate to these pictures and make some model farm and factory buildings. When you have assembled a reasonable collection, set up a display table showing farming activities. Change the display each day by taking away one or two farm items and replacing them with industrial buildings and vehicles. By the end of a week the display should be almost, but not quite, covered with factories. Talk about the changes as they happen. Get the children to make a diary, or draw simple plans and pictures, of the different scenes. Can any children think of places nearby where something similar has happened? Reinforce the work using **Copymaster 5.19** (Spot the Difference).

Activity 5.37: Change in your local area

Materials needed

Old photographs and postcards of the place where you live, simple maps and plans.

Make a collection of old photographs and postcards of the place where you live. Ask the children to bring in pictures which their parents or grandparents have collected. Find out if there are any books with collections of historic photographs of your area. Have any been reproduced in local newspapers? Put the pictures up as a display and link them to a street plan or map. See if you can find any old maps showing how your settlement has grown. Ask elderly people to come and see your exhibition and talk about what they remember from the past. Dress for a day in Victorian costume. Talk about things which would have been different in those times. Would your school have existed? How many local buildings would have been built? Make pictures of some different scenes from the past.

Activity 5.38: Obsolete objects

Materials needed

A range of obsolete items and their modern equivalents.

Make a display of objects which are old-fashioned or obsolete. Talk about each one with the children. What was it used for? How was it used? Why is it no longer needed? Try to group the items together. For example, all the things which were used in the home could be put into one area, while tools and equipment for workmen could be put into another. Talk about the modern equivalents for each item and add them to your display if possible. How many things used to be worked by hand but are now powered by electricity? Make a survey of electrical goods in school. Where are the sockets? How does the electricity get from place to place? Talk about where electricity comes from, the impact of power lines on the environment and the problems that power stations cause.

Activity 5.39: New things

Materials needed

Sticky paper, scissors.

Go for a walk around your school. Try to decide what has changed recently. Are there any new displays? Which books have been added to the library? Have any repairs been done? This exercise is a useful way of developing the children's observational skills and it illustrates how the school environment is always changing. You could get the children to cut out some stickers or stars to fix on to the things they have

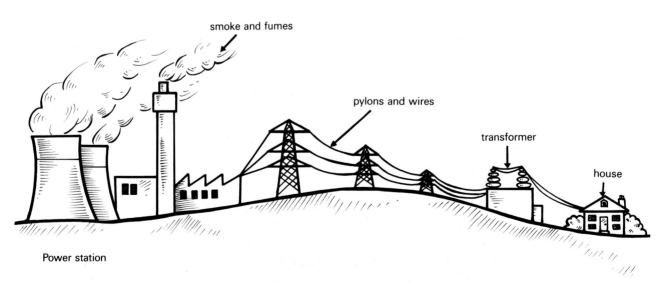

Power station

How electricity reaches our homes

discovered. Back in the classroom they could make a list of all the things they remember.

sticky paper

Activity 5.40: Door walk

Materials needed
Rectangles of white card, artwork materials.

Go for a walk around some local streets to look at front doors. In what ways are they different? Why do people replace their front doors? Which ones look best? Give the children some rectangles of white card and ask them to design a front door of their own. Alternatively, you could use **Copymaster 5.20** (Front Doors) to make a frieze. Get the children to look at the school front door. How does it contribute to the appearance of the building? Could it be improved in any way?

Activity 5.41: Advertisements

Make a survey of advertisements in your local area. Where can you find them? Plan a walk linking together advertisements in shop windows and on hoardings, walls and lamp posts. What different things are advertised? Do advertisements spoil the view, or do they hide a messy place? What advertisements are there in your school? Have they been there a long time, and do they need replacing?

Activity 5.42: Favourite building

Materials needed
Clipboards, drawing paper, camera, binoculars.

Discuss different buildings near your school with the children, and choose one which they like. Organise a short outing to visit and study it in detail. Get the children to make drawings of the building from different angles. See that they look especially closely at the windows, doors, roof and decorations. You could take a pair of binoculars to help them make out the details. Photographs can also help to record information and are useful in any class display. Discuss how

the building contributes to the environment. What would the children feel if someone decided to knock it down? Get the class to design and draw some buildings of their own. What sort of place would they put them in? Would they be suitable for a hill top, a valley, a large open space or a city high street?

Activity 5.43: Wear and tear

Materials needed
Card, scissors.

Examine the school buildings and grounds to look for examples of wear and tear. Examples might include flaking paintwork, broken roof tiles, cracks in the wall, trampled grass, worn verges and scratched brickwork. Help the children to spot these different things by making a simple 'looking eye' from card. When you get back to the classroom ask the children to write a sentence about each one. You could mount their work with the looking eye over the top like a frame. Discuss what has caused the damage.

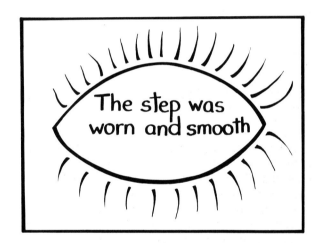

'Looking eye' made from card

Copymasters

5.17 Things which Change   Use this copymaster to help introduce the idea of change. The examples on the sheet start with change in the natural world but go on to illustrate the impact of human action.

5.18 Change Dial   The children should make a set of four drawings in the empty spaces. These could illustrate changes in the weather, changes in plants and animals or changes in the environment. Activity 5.35 describes how to use the pictures in a dial.

5.19 Spot the Difference   The two drawings show how industry can affect the countryside. Children could either circle the differences or use the drawings as a colouring sheet.

5.20 Front Doors   Three different front doors are illustrated in this copymaster. When the children have coloured the drawings they could cut them out for a class frieze.

IMPROVE THE ENVIRONMENT

CM 5.21 –5.25

Statement of Attainment

Level 2

2c) Pupils should be able to suggest how they could improve the quality of their own environment.

Example and links with the Programme of Study

If possible, children should undertake a practical activity. This might involve a school improvement project, such as setting up a garden or nature area. Alternatively, the children could be involved in a scheme to collect waste paper or steel and aluminium drink cans for recycling.

Introduction

The Geography Working Group identified environmental issues as an important element of geography. They made it clear that the curriculum should help children 'develop an informed concern about the quality of the environment' and thus 'enhance their sense of responsibility for the care of the Earth.' (Final Report, paragraph 4.6.) One of the best ways of doing this is through practical activities.

Most children feel that they have very little power over their surroundings. Even adults tend to feel there is very little they can do about the great environmental issues facing the world. Yet it is our individual actions that can collectively solve or compound the problems that we face. Children need to realise that what they do *does* have an effect on the world, and they should be taught to look after their environment.

One way of illustrating this idea is to consider the places that children are allowed to visit within the school building and the things they are allowed to do. Are there any rules governing their behaviour? How could other children spoil their enjoyment? You could then go on to examine natural habitats in the school and local area and discuss possible improvements.

Key vocabulary

animal	improve
attractive	nature
beautiful	plants
bird	playground
earth	recycle
environment	school
garden	surroundings
habitat	wildlife

Key questions

What are you allowed to do?
What are you not allowed to do?
How could you improve your environment?
Which grown-ups help to improve the environment?
What do they do?

Picture books

The Hurricane Tree by Libby Purves (Bodley, 1988) tells the story of what happened in the hurricane of October 1987, and how the damage was repaired. *Nowhere to Play* by Kurusa (Black, 1981) is another true story. It describes how children struggled to find a playground in a South American city. For a more light-hearted approach you might read the children 'A House is Built for Eeyore at Pooh Corner' from *The House at Pooh Corner* by A.A. Milne.

Rhyme

Mary, Mary, Quite Contrary

'Mary, Mary, quite contrary,
How does your garden grow?'
'With silver bells and cockle shells,
And pretty maids all in a row'.

Activity 5.44: Classroom improvements

Materials needed

Home improvement magazines, furniture catalogues, samples of wallpaper and curtain materials.

Ask the children how they would redesign or redecorate the classroom. What colours would they use for the paintwork? Would they add a carpet or wallpaper? What style of furniture would they choose? Make up an 'improvements book' with samples of materials, advertisements for paint types and pictures from furniture catalogues.

Activity 5.45: School improvements

Materials needed

Simple plan of the school.

Explore your school with the class and decide on any changes they would make. Make a list of ideas using the headings: 'new paint', 'carpets', 'flowers' and 'pictures'. Using **Copymaster 5.21** (School Improvements), get the children to make signs to place around the school at the places they have selected. Give each sign a code and plot it on a simple outline map of the school. Get the children to explain each idea in greater detail in an accompanying 'improvements manual' as a follow-up exercise. (Further ideas on the school improvements theme are suggested in Activity 5.46.)

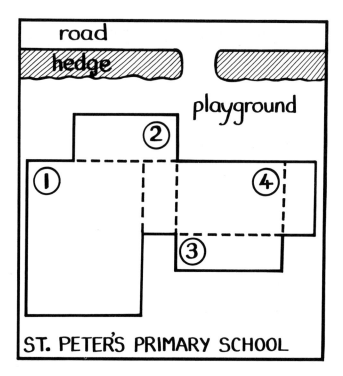

School improvements plan

Improvements manual

Activity 5.46: Dream ideas

Materials needed
Class display book, photographs of individual children.

Many of the ideas which the children will suggest for improvements are likely to be rather unrealistic. You could make a collection of these suggestions in a book of dream ideas. Examples might include a sweet shop in the playground or a time travel capsule. If you add a drawing or a small photograph of the child next to each suggestion it will help to give the book a distinctive identity.

Activity 5.47: Plans for the future
Arrange for the headteacher or chairperson of the governors to visit the class and talk about what they would like to do to improve the school. Are there big and small projects? What could be done soon, and what will take many years to achieve? Is there anything which could be done at no cost at all? Will outsiders be needed to help make the improvements? How can the children help?

Activity 5.48: The outside view
Look at two different views of your school. Using **Copymaster 5.23** (Different Views), get the children to decide which view they prefer. Discuss how they would improve the view they do not like. What are the things which spoil it? What could be added to create interest? Would it be possible to add colour or vegetation? Get the children to make paintings of the improvements they would like to see made.

Activity 5.49: Wildlife area

Materials needed
Logs, stones, flower pots, old bricks, dustbin lid.

Improve the environment for small creatures by building a wildlife area. Find a suitable place in the school grounds and count the number of creatures you can find. Record the results on **Copymaster 5.24** (Wildlife Survey). Add some stones, logs, flower pots on their side and old bricks with gaps in between them. If possible, include an upturned dustbin lid. Keep watch on the area and make a survey of the wildlife at suitable intervals, such as a week or a month. What changes do

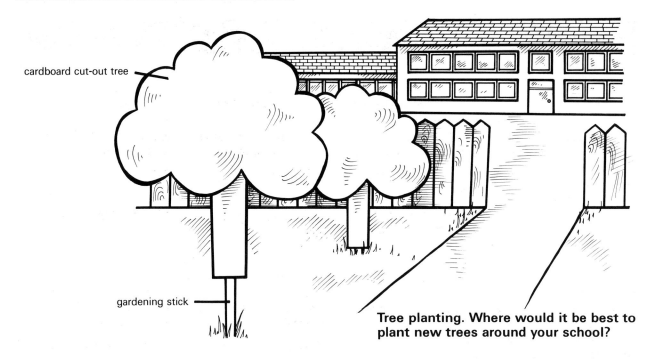

cardboard cut-out tree

gardening stick

Tree planting. Where would it be best to plant new trees around your school?

you notice? Does your project appear to have benefited wildlife?

Activity 5.50: Tree planting

Materials needed
Cardboard, gardening sticks, Sellotape.

Take a careful look at the school grounds and decide where it might be useful to plant some new trees. Get the children to make some cardboard cut-out trees using a template. Fix the trees to gardening sticks with glue or sellotape and 'plant' them in the places the children have selected.

Activity 5.51: Recycling scheme
Set up a recycling scheme for waste paper or aluminium cans. Establish a collecting point somewhere in the classroom and record the amount of material brought in each day. You could weigh the amount of paper or count the number of cans and show the results on a bar chart. Arrange for the material to be collected after a month or at the end of term. How much money has it raised? What will it be spent on? Find out about the recycling process from reference books and discuss what other materials can be used again. **Copymaster 5.25** (Recycling) is designed to help children record their ideas.

Activity 5.52: Improvements in the local area
Go for a walk in your local area and note down any improvements that you notice. Look for new doors, windows, garages and driveways. Are there any new signs, paths or play equipment in the local park? What are people doing to look after the environment? Discuss ways in which further improvements might be made and write to the local council planning department with your ideas.

Activity 5.53: Working for the environment
Make a list of people who work to improve or look after the environment. Examples include painters and decorators, builders, gardeners, architects and designers. Think also about people who work to improve conditions for poor people, either in this country or abroad. Some children may have heard of agencies such as Oxfam and Save the Children. Find out about environmental organisations such as Greenpeace and Friends of the Earth. What do they do? Write to them and ask them to send leaflets and information for the children to study. Why is their work important?

Copymasters

5.21 School Improvements This copymaster provides outline drawings which the children can colour and cut out to make signs. It is best to reproduce the copymaster on light card if possible.

5.22 Patterns The aim of this sheet is to encourage children to look at patterns around their school. They may not find all the examples illustrated but they should begin to think about how patterns improve the environment.

5.23 Different Views This copymaster will help children to compare two different views of their school and consider the factors that make an attractive scene. You should check that the children understand all the terms before they start the activity.

5.24 Wildlife Survey The children will need this copymaster when they record the variety of creatures in the wildlife area. They should put a tick or tally mark for each creature they discover.

5.25 Recycling Children should write down different examples of things which can be recycled in the empty spaces on this copymaster. They could then go on to find out more about the process involved.

WORKING TOWARDS LEVEL 3 ▶

Programme of Study	School-based work	Contrasting area	World dimension
Pupils should be taught how the extraction of natural resources affects environments, for example, quarries, mining.	What natural resources are used in your school? Where do they come from? What damage does this do to the environment?	Are there any mines or quarries nearby? What effect do they have on the environment? (E.g. open gravel pits, scars in hillsides and slag heaps.) How have people tried to deal with these problems?	Which parts of the world produce natural resources? How are they obtained? Why are they useful?
Pupils should be taught the difference between manufactured goods and natural resources.	What manufactured goods do you use in your classroom? What are they made from? Are there any handmade goods?	Are there any factories nearby? What do they make? Where do the raw materials come from?	Where are the world's industrial areas? What are multinational companies? Does everybody use manufactured goods?
Pupils should be taught about activities intended to improve the environment in the local area or in a place they have visited.	Has your school building been repaired or improved recently? What is done to look after the school garden? Is your school or class involved in any recycling projects?	Are people trying to improve streets and buildings nearby? Are there any museums or heritage centres in your area? Are there any parks or nature reserves?	What different projects around the world are intended to conserve the environment? Who organises them? Are they successful?

131

Atlases

Customer Services
Collins Longman Atlases
Longman Group UK Ltd
Harlow
Essex
CM19 4BR

Charts

Pictorial Charts Educational Trust
27 Kirchen Road
London
W13 0UD

Developing countries

Centre for World Development Education
1 Catton Street
London
WC1R 4AB

Oxfam
274 Banbury Road
Oxford
OX2 7GZ

Save the Children
Mary Datchelor House
17 Grove Lane
Camberwell
London
SE5 8RD

Environmental issues

Centre for Alternative Technology
Llwngern Quarry
Machynlleth
Powys
SY20 9AZ

Friends of the Earth
26–28 Underwood Street
London
N1 7JQ

Greenpeace
30–31 Islington Green
London
N1 8XE

World Wide Fund for Nature
Weysdie Park
Godalming
Surrey
GU17 1XP

Globes and compasses

N.E.S. Arnold
Ludlow Hill Road
West Bridgfield
Nottingham
NG2 6HD

Hope Education
Orb Mill
Huddersfield Road
Waterhead
Oldham
OL4 2ST

Inflatable Globes

Cambridge Publishing Services Ltd
PO Box 62
Cambridge
CB3 9NA

Journals

Primary Geographer
Geographical Association
343 Fulwood Road
Sheffield
S10 3BP

Maps

Information and Publications
Ordnance Survey
Romsey Road
Southampton
SO9 4DH